U·X·L
Encyclopedia
of Science

U·X·L

Encyclopedia

of Science

Second Edition

Volume 9: Re-St

Rob Nagel, Editor

GALE GROUP

THOMSON LEARNING

Detroit • New York • San Diego • San Francisco
Boston • New Haven, Conn. • Waterville, Maine
London • Munich

U·X·L
Encyclopedia of Science
Second Edition

Rob Nagel, *Editor*

Staff

Elizabeth Shaw Grunow, *U•X•L Editor*

Julie Carnagie, *Contributing Editor*

Carol DeKane Nagel, *U•X•L Managing Editor*

Thomas L. Romig, *U•X•L Publisher*

Shalice Shah-Caldwell, *Permissions Associate (Pictures)*

Robyn Young, *Imaging and Multimedia Content Editor*

Rita Wimberley, *Senior Buyer*

Pamela A. E. Galbreath, *Senior Art Designe*r

Michelle Cadorée, *Indexing*

GGS Information Services, *Typesetting*

On the front cover: Nikola Tesla with one of his generators, reproduced by permission of the Granger Collection.

On the back cover: The flow of red blood cells through blood vessels, reproduced by permission of Phototake.

Library of Congress Cataloging-in-Publication Data

U-X-L encyclopedia of science.—2nd ed. / Rob Nagel, editor
    p.cm.
    Includes bibliographical references and indexes.
    Contents: v.1. A-As — v.2. At-Car — v.3. Cat-Cy — v.4. D-Em — v.5. En-G — v.6. H-Mar — v.7. Mas-O — v.8. P-Ra — v.9. Re-St — v.10. Su-Z.
    Summary: Includes 600 topics in the life, earth, and physical sciences as well as in engineering, technology, math, environmental science, and psychology.
    ISBN 0-7876-5432-9 (set : acid-free paper) — ISBN 0-7876-5433-7 (v.1 : acid-free paper) — ISBN 0-7876-5434-5 (v.2 : acid-free paper) — ISBN 0-7876-5435-3 (v.3 : acid-free paper) — ISBN 0-7876-5436-1 (v.4 : acid-free paper) — ISBN 0-7876-5437-X (v.5 : acid-free paper) — ISBN 0-7876-5438-8 (v.6 : acid-free paper) — ISBN 0-7876-5439-6 (v.7 : acid-free paper) — ISBN 0-7876-5440-X (v.8 : acid-free paper) — ISBN 0-7876-5441-8 (v.9 : acid-free paper) — ISBN 0-7876-5775-1 (v.10 : acid-free paper)
    1. Science-Encyclopedias, Juvenile. 2. Technology-Encyclopedias, Juvenile. [1. Science-Encyclopedias. 2. Technology-Encyclopedias.] I. Title: UXL encyclopedia of science. II. Nagel, Rob.
    Q121.U18 2001
    503-dc21
                                                                2001035562

Printed in the United States of America

10 9 8 7 6 5 4 3 2 1

Table of Contents

Contents

Reader's Guide

Demystify scientific theories, controversies, discoveries, and phenomena with the *U•X•L Encyclopedia of Science,* Second Edition.

This alphabetically organized ten-volume set opens up the entire world of science in clear, nontechnical language. More than 600 entries—an increase of more than 10 percent from the first edition—provide fascinating facts covering the entire spectrum of science. This second edition features more than 50 new entries and more than 100 updated entries. These informative essays range from 250 to 2,500 words, many of which include helpful sidebar boxes that highlight fascinating facts and phenomena. Topics profiled are related to the physical, life, and earth sciences, as well as to math, psychology, engineering, technology, and the environment.

In addition to solid information, the *Encyclopedia* also provides these features:

- "Words to Know" boxes that define commonly used terms
- Extensive cross references that lead directly to related entries
- A table of contents by scientific field that organizes the entries
- More than 600 color and black-and-white photos and technical drawings
- Sources for further study, including books, magazines, and Web sites

Each volume concludes with a cumulative subject index, making it easy to locate quickly the theories, people, objects, and inventions discussed throughout the *U•X•L Encyclopedia of Science,* Second Edition.

Suggestions

We welcome any comments on this work and suggestions for entries to feature in future editions of *U•X•L Encyclopedia of Science*. Please write: Editors, *U•X•L Encyclopedia of Science,* U•X•L, Gale Group, 27500 Drake Road, Farmington Hills, Michigan, 48331-3535; call toll-free: 800-877-4253; fax to: 248-699-8097; or send an e-mail via www.galegroup.com.

Entries by Scientific Field

Boldface indicates volume numbers.

Acoustics

Acoustics	**1**:17
Compact disc	**3**:531
Diffraction	**4**:648
Echolocation	**4**:720
Magnetic recording/ audiocassette	**6**:1209
Sonar	**9**:1770
Ultrasonics	**10**:1941
Video recording	**10**:1968

Aerodynamics

Aerodynamics	**1**:39
Fluid dynamics	**5**:882

Aeronautical engineering

Aircraft	**1**:74
Atmosphere observation	**2**:215
Balloon	**1**:261
Jet engine	**6**:1143
Rockets and missiles	**9**:1693

Aerospace engineering

International Ultraviolet Explorer	**6**:1120
Rockets and missiles	**9**:1693
Satellite	**9**:1707
Spacecraft, manned	**9**:1777
Space probe	**9**:1783
Space station, international	**9**:1788
Telescope	**10**:1869

Agriculture

Agriculture	**1**:62
Agrochemical	**1**:65
Aquaculture	**1**:166
Biotechnology	**2**:309
Cotton	**3**:577
Crops	**3**:582
DDT (dichlorodiphenyl- trichloroethane)	**4**:619
Drift net	**4**:680
Forestry	**5**:901
Genetic engineering	**5**:973
Organic farming	**7**:1431
Slash-and-burn agriculture	**9**:1743
Soil	**9**:1758

Anatomy and physiology

Anatomy	**1**:138
Blood	**2**:326

Astrophysics

Biology

Embryology

Engineering

Entomology

Reaction, chemical

When a chemical reaction occurs, at least one product is formed that is different from the substances present before the change occurred. As an example, it is possible to pass an electric current through a sample of water and obtain a mixture of oxygen and hydrogen gases. That change is a chemical reaction because neither oxygen nor hydrogen were present as elements before the change took place.

Any chemical change involves two sets of substances: reactants and products. A reactant is an element or compound present before a chemical change takes place. In the example above, only one reactant was present: water. A product is an element or compound formed as a result of the chemical reaction. In the preceding example, both hydrogen and oxygen are products of the reaction.

Chemical reactions are represented by means of chemical equations. A chemical equation is a symbolic statement that represents the changes that occur during a chemical reaction. The statement consists of the symbols of the elements and the formulas of the products and reactants, along with other symbols that represent certain conditions present in the reaction. For example, the arrow (or yields) sign, →, separates the reactants from the products in a reaction. The chemical equation that represents the electrolysis of water is $2 H_2O \rightarrow 2 H_2 + O_2$.

Types of chemical reactions

Most chemical reactions can be categorized into one of about five general types: synthesis, decomposition, single replacement, double replacement, and oxidation-reduction. A miscellaneous category is also needed for reactions that do not fit into one of these five categories.

Characteristics of each type.

Synthesis: Two substances combine to form one new substance:

In general: $A + B \rightarrow AB$

For example:

$$2\,Na + Cl_2 \rightarrow 2\,NaCl \text{ or } CaO + H_2O \rightarrow Ca(OH)_2$$

Decomposition: One substance breaks down to form two new substances:

In general: $AB \rightarrow A + B$

For example:

$$2\,H_2O \rightarrow 2\,H_2 + O_2$$

Single Replacement: An element and a compound react such that the element replaces one other element in the compound:

In general: $A + BC \rightarrow AC + B$

For example:

$$Mg + 2\,HCl \rightarrow MgCl_2 + H_2$$

Double Replacement: Two compounds react with each other in such a way that they exchange partners with each other:

In general: $AB + CD \rightarrow AD + CB$

For example:

$$NaBr + HCl \rightarrow NaCl + HBr$$

Oxidation-reduction: One or more elements in the reaction changes its oxidation state during the reaction:

In general: $A^{3+} \rightarrow A^{6+}$

For example:

$$Cr^{3+} \rightarrow Cr^{6+}$$

Energy changes and chemical kinetics

Chemical reactions are typically accompanied by energy changes. The equation for the synthesis of ammonia from its elements is $N_2 + 3\,H_2 \rightarrow 2\,NH_3$, but that reaction takes place only under very special conditions—namely at a high temperature and pressure and in the presence of a catalyst. Energy changes that occur during chemical reactions are the subject of a field of science known as thermodynamics.

In addition, chemical reactions are often a good deal more complex than a chemical equation might lead one to believe. For example, one can write the equation for the synthesis of hydrogen iodide from its elements, as follows: $H_2 + I_2 \rightarrow 2\,HI$. In fact, chemists know that this reaction does not take place in a single step. Instead, it occurs in a series of reactions in which hydrogen and iodine atoms react with each other one at a time. The final equation, $H_2 + I_2 \rightarrow 2\,HI$, is actually no more than a summary of the net result of all those reactions. The field of chemistry that deals with the details of chemical reactions is known as chemical kinetics.

Reaction of sulfuric acid and sugar. The acid dehydrates the sugar forming a pillar of carbon (black) and steam. *(Reproduced by permission of Photo Researchers, Inc.)*

Recycling

Recycling is a method of reusing materials that would otherwise be disposed of in a landfill or incinerator. Household products that contain glass, aluminum, paper, and plastic are used for recycling and to make new products. Recycling has many benefits: it saves money in production and energy costs, helps save the environment from the impacts of extracting and processing virgin (never used; not altered by human activity) materials, and means that there is less trash that needs to be disposed.

The concept of recycling is not a new one. At the beginning of the twentieth century, 70 percent of the nation's cities had programs to recycle one or more specific materials. During World War II (1939–45), 25 percent of the waste generated by industrial processes was recycled and reused. Since the general public has become more environmentally conscious, the recycling rate in the United States has risen from 7 percent in 1960 to 17 percent in 1990 to 28 percent in 2000. Analysts predict that by 2005, Americans will be recycling and composting at least 83 tons (75 metric tons) or 35 percent of all municipal waste.

Curbside collection of recyclable household wastes in Livonia, Michigan. This municipality, and many others, orders that glass, newsprint, steel cans, and certain kinds of plastics be recycled. Recyclable wastes are collected in bins provided by the city. *(Reproduced by permission of Field Mark Publications.)*

Process

Recycling is a three-step process. The first step involves collecting and reprocessing materials for recycling. These materials must be separated from other trash and prepared to become new products. Manufacturing of new products from recycled materials is the second step. The final step is the consumer's purchase and use of the recycled product.

Some problems with recycling

These steps may appear to constitute a simple and straightforward process, but such is not the case. A number of basic questions have to be resolved before recycling of solid wastes can become a practical reality. Some of these questions are technological. For example, there is currently no known way to recycle certain types of widely used plastics in an economical way. There is no problem in collecting these plastics and separating them from trash, but the process stops there. No one has found a method for re-melting the plastics and then converting them into new products.

A second problem is economic. Suppose that it costs more to make a new product out of recycled materials than out of new materials. What

Glass containers ready for recycling. *(Reproduced by permission of Field Mark Publications.)*

company is willing to lose money by using recycled, rather than new, materials?

Legislation

One way to expand the use of recycling, of course, is to invent more efficient technologies to deal with waste materials. Another approach, however, is to use the power of government to encourage or even require recycling. Governments are interested in promoting recycling because the cost of other means of solid waste disposal is often very high. If citizens can be made to recycle waste materials rather than to just throw them away, governments can save money on sanitary landfills, incinerators, and other means of waste disposal.

Both the U.S. federal government and individual states have now passed a number of laws relating to recycling. For example, a number of states states (including Arizona, California, Connecticut, Illinois, Maryland, Missouri, North Carolina, Oregon, Rhode Island, Texas, and Wisconsin) and the District of Columbia require that newspapers published in their jurisdictions have a minimum content of recycled fiber.

On the federal level, the Environmental Protection Agency (EPA) requires government agencies to set aside a portion of their budgets to buy recycled products. All agencies are required to purchase recycled paper, refined oil, building insulation made with recycled material, and other items that are made from recycled products.

Government regulations, however, are not necessarily the best possible answer to developing recycling policies. For one thing, prices are usually higher for recycled products, and there may be problems with availability and quality of recycled goods.

Overall, researchers and environmentalists tend to agree that creativity will be the key to solving many of our solid waste disposal problems. Many landfills have reached their carrying capacity. In 1978, there were roughly 14,000 landfills in the United States. By 2000, that number had dropped to just over 5,000. Many of those currently open are expected to be closed within a few years. Fresh Kills Landfill on Staten Island, New York, was the largest landfill in the world. It covered over 2,200 acres (880 hectares) and reached a height taller than the Statue of Liberty. Open in 1948, it was finally closed in March 2001. As we continue to run out of space to put solid waste, recycling, composting, and reusing are fast becoming environmental and economic necessities to help reduce some of that waste.

[*See also* **Composting; Waste management**]

Red giant

A red giant is a star that has exhausted the primary supply of hydrogen fuel at its core. An average-sized star like our Sun will spend the final 10 percent of its life as a red giant. In this phase, a star's surface temperature drops to between 3,140 and 6,741°F (1,727 and 3,727°C) and its diameter expands to 10 to 1,000 times that of the Sun. The star takes on a reddish color, which is what gives it its name.

With no hydrogen left at the core of a star to fuel the nuclear reaction that keeps it burning, the core begins to contract. The core's contracting releases gravitational energy into the surrounding regions of the star, causing it to expand. Consequently, the outer layers cool down and the color of the star (which is a function of temperature) becomes red. The star may slowly shrink and expand more than once as it evolves into a red giant.

This change marks the start of a dynamic process in which the star develops into a variable star. It becomes alternately brighter and dimmer, generally spending about one year in each phase. The star continues in a variable state until it completely runs out of fuel.

Words to Know

Black hole: Remains of a massive star that has burned out its nuclear fuel and collapsed under tremendous gravitational force into a single point of infinite mass and gravity.

Fusion: Combining of nuclei of two or more lighter elements into one nucleus of a heavier element; the process stars use to produce energy to support themselves against their own gravity.

Nebula: A cloud of interstellar dust and gas.

Neutron star: Extremely dense, compact, neutron-filled remains of a star following a supernova.

Variable star: Star that varies in brightness over periods of time ranging from hours to years.

White dwarf: Cooling, shrunken core remaining after a medium-sized star ceases to burn.

While the star is in a puffed-up state, helium continues to accumulate at its core. Since the helium initially is not hot enough to undergo fusion (the process by which two atoms combine, releasing a vast amount of energy), it becomes denser and denser. Finally, pressure alone forces the atoms to fuse, forming carbon and oxygen. At the same time, the core shrinks and the star becomes bluer and smaller.

Using helium as a fuel, the star's core continues to burn normally for a while, although the star shines less brightly than it did in its expanded state. At the same time, any remaining hydrogen in regions farther out from the core fuse into helium. The core becomes so hot that it may pulsate (vary in brightness). This stage does not last long, however, since the helium burns quickly.

As the helium runs out, the star again puffs up—this time to about 500 times the size of the Sun, with about 5,000 times the brightness of the Sun. Buried deep inside the star's unstable atmosphere is a hot core about the size of Earth, but with 60 percent of the Sun's mass. As a final act, the atmosphere dislodges from the core and floats off as a planetary nebula (cloud). The glowing core, called a white dwarf, is left to cool for eternity.

More massive stars exit the red giant stage with a bang, transformed by a supernova (explosion) into a neutron star (dense, neutron-filled remains of a star) or a black hole (a single point of infinite mass and gravity).

[*See also* **Star; White dwarf**]

Redshift

In astronomy, when matter moves away from an observation point, its light spectrum displays a redshift. A redshift is one type of Doppler effect. Named for Austrian physicist Christian Johann Doppler (1803–1853), this principle states that if a light (or sound) source is moving away from a given point, its wavelengths (distance between two peaks of a wave) will be lengthened. Conversely, if an object emitting light or sound is moving toward that point, its wavelengths will be shortened.

With light, longer wavelengths stretch to the red end of the color spectrum while shorter wavelengths bunch up at the blue end. The shortening of wavelengths of an approaching object is called a blueshift.

The first astronomer to observe a space object's Doppler shift was American astronomer Vesto Melvin Slipher (1875–1969) in 1912. His

Words to Know

Blueshift: The Doppler shift observed when a celestial object is moving closer to Earth.

Doppler effect: The change in wavelength and frequency (number of vibrations per second) of either light or sound as the source is moving either towards or away from the observer.

Redshift: The Doppler shift observed when a celestial object is moving farther away from Earth.

Spectrum: Range of individual wavelengths of radiation produced when light is broken down into its component colors.

Speed of light: Speed at which light travels in a vacuum: approximately 186,000 miles (299,000 kilometers) per second.

Wavelength: The distance between two peaks in any wave.

subject was the Andromeda galaxy, which was then believed to be a nebula, or a cloud of dust and gas (at that time it was not known there were other galaxies beyond the Milky Way). Slipher discovered that the spectrum of Andromeda was shifted toward the blue end, meaning that it was approaching Earth.

Two years later, Slipher analyzed the spectra of fourteen other spiral nebula and found that only two were blueshifted, while twelve were redshifted. The redshifts he observed for some spirals implied they were moving at enormous speeds.

Hubble and the expanding universe

An extremely important finding relating to redshifts was made in 1929 by Edwin Hubble (1889–1953), the American astronomer who first proved the existence of other galaxies. Together with his colleague Milton Humason, Hubble photographed distant galaxies and discovered that their spectra were all shifted toward the red wavelengths of light. Further study showed a relationship between the degree of redshift and that object's distance from Earth. In other words, the greater an object's redshift, the more distant it is and the faster it is moving away from Earth.

The large degree of redshift in the spectra of these galaxies suggested that they were moving away from Earth at a phenomenal rate. Humason found some galaxies moving at one-seventh the speed of light.

Hubble and Humason's research on redshifts led to two important conclusions: every galaxy is moving away from every other galaxy and, therefore, the universe is expanding.

[*See also* **Binary star; Doppler effect; Electromagnetic spectrum; Galaxy; Star**]

Artist's impression of a binary star system consisting of a black hole and a red giant star. A binary star system has two sets of spectral lines that are alternately red and blue shifted. This indicates that while one star is traveling away from Earth (redshift), the other is coming toward it (blueshift). *(Reproduced by permission of Photo Researchers, Inc.)*

Reinforcement, positive and negative

In psychology, reinforcement refers to the procedure of presenting or removing a stimulus to maintain or increase the likelihood of a behavioral response. (A stimulus is something that causes a response.) Reinforcement is usually divided into two types: positive and negative.

If a stimulus is presented immediately after a behavior and that stimulus increases the probability that the behavior will occur again, the stimulus is called a positive reinforcer. Giving a child candy for cleaning his or her room is an example of a positive reinforcer. The child will learn to clean his or her room (behavior) more often in the future, believing he or she will receive something positive—the candy (stimulus)—in return.

Like positive reinforcement, negative reinforcement increases the likelihood that a behavior associated with it will be continued. However, a negative reinforcer is an unpleasant stimulus that is removed after a behavioral response. Negative reinforcers can range from uncomfortable physical sensations to actions causing severe physical distress. Taking aspirin for a headache is an example of negative reinforcement. If a person's headache (stimulus) goes away after taking aspirin (behavior), then it is likely that the person will take aspirin for headaches in the future.

Reinforcers can also be further classified as primary and secondary. Primary reinforcers are natural; they are not learned. They usually satisfy basic biological needs, such as food, air, water, and shelter. Secondary reinforcers are those that have come to be associated with primary reinforcers. Since money can be used to satisfy the basic needs of food, clothing, and shelter, it is known as a secondary reinforcer. Secondary reinforcers are also called conditioned reinforcers.

Classical conditioning

Reinforcement as a theoretical concept in psychology can be traced back to Russian scientist Ivan P. Pavlov (1849–1936), who studied conditioning and learning in animals in the early 1900s. Pavlov developed the general procedures and terminology for studying what is now called classical conditioning. While studying the salivary functions of dogs, Pavlov noticed that they began to salivate just before he began to feed them. He concluded that salivating in anticipation of the food was a learned response. To further prove this theory, Pavlov conducted an experiment. Just before he gave a dog food, Pavlov rang a bell. After pairing the bell and

Words to Know

Classical conditioning: A type of conditioning or learning in which a stimulus that brings about a behavioral response is paired with a neutral stimulus until that neutral stimulus brings about the response by itself.

Operant conditioning: A type of conditioning or learning in which a person or animal learns to perform or not perform a particular behavior based on its positive or negative consequences.

Primary reinforcers: Stimuli such as food, water, and shelter that satisfy basic needs.

Secondary reinforcers: Stimuli that have come to provide reinforcement through their association with primary reinforcers.

Stimulus: Something that causes a behavioral response.

food several times, Pavlov just rang the bell. He discovered that the sound of the bell alone was enough to make the dogs salivate.

Pavlov labeled the food an unconditional stimulus because it reliably (unconditionally) led to salivation. He called the salivation an unconditional response. The bell tone was a conditioned stimulus because the dog did not salivate in response to the bell until he had been conditioned to do so through repeated pairings with the food. The salivation in response to the bell became a conditioned response.

Classical conditioning thus occurs when a person or animal forms an association between two events. One event need not immediately follow the other. What is important is that one event predicts or brings about the other. An example of classical conditioning in humans can be seen in a trip to the dentist's office. On a person's first visit, the sound of the drill signifies nothing to that person until the dentist begins to use the drill. The pain and discomfort of having a tooth drilled is then remembered by that person on the subsequent visit. The sound of the drill is enough to produce a feeling of anxiety, tensed muscles, and sweaty palms in that person even before the dentist has begun to use the drill.

Operant conditioning

In classical conditioning, the learned responses are reflexes, such as salivating or sweating. The stimuli (food or a dentist's drill) bring about these responses automatically. In operant conditioning, the learned behavioral responses are voluntary. A person or animal learns to perform or not perform a particular behavior based on its positive or negative consequences.

American behavioral psychologist B. F. Skinner (1904–1990) conducted experiments during the 1930s and 1940s to prove that human and animal behavior is based not on independent motivation but on response to reward and punishment. Skinner designed an enclosed, soundproof box equipped with tools, levers, and other devices. In this box, which came to be called the Skinner box, he taught rats to push buttons, pull strings, and press levers to receive a food or water reward.

This type of procedure and the resultant conditioning have become known as operant conditioning. The term "operant" refers to behaviors that respond to, or operate on, the surrounding environment. From his experiments, Skinner developed the theory that humans are controlled (stimulated) solely by forces in their environment. Rewarded behavior (positive reinforcement) is encouraged, and unrewarded behavior (negative reinforcement) is terminated.

[*See also* **Behavior**]

Relativity, theory of

The theory of relativity is an approach for studying the nature of the universe. It was devised by German-born American physicist Albert Einstein (1879–1955) in the first quarter of the twentieth century. The theory is usually separated into two parts: the special theory and the general theory. The outlines of the special theory were first published by Einstein in 1905 and dealt with physical systems in uniform velocity. (The term velocity refers both to the speed with which an object is moving and to the direction in which it is moving.) The theory applies, for example, to physical events that might take place in a railroad train traveling down a track at a constant 50 miles (80 kilometers) per hour.

The general theory was announced by Einstein in 1915. It deals with physical systems in accelerated motion—that is, in systems whose velocity is constantly changing. The general theory could be used to describe events taking place in a railroad train that accelerates from a speed of 50 miles (80 kilometers) per hour to 100 miles (140 kilometers) per hour. Obviously, the general theory applies to a larger category of events than does the special theory and, therefore, has many more applications.

Classical physics

The term classical physics is used to describe a whole set of concepts and beliefs about the natural world held by physicists prior to about 1900. According to classical physics, every effect could be traced to some specific and identifiable cause. If an apple fell out of a tree, then that effect could be traced to some specific cause—in this case, gravitational attraction.

Also, physicists believed that physical objects had constant properties that did not change unless they were altered or destroyed. For example, suppose that you had a meter stick that was exactly 1.000 meter long. You could trust that meter stick to find the correct length of a line whether you made the measurement in your laboratory at the university or in an airplane flying at 500 miles (800 kilometers) per hour above Earth's surface.

Relative motion

Even before 1900, though, a few physicists had begun to question some of these assumptions. These physicists based their questions on some very obvious points. Consider, for example, the following scenario: two railroad train cars are traveling next to each other at the same speed. In such a case, a person in one train could look into the windows of the second train and observe the passengers in its cars. To the observer seated in the first train, it appears as if the second train is at rest.

Suppose the second train begins to speed up or slow down. In that case, it seems to be moving slowly away from the first train—forward or backward—perhaps at the rate of a few miles (kilometers) per hour. In reality, though, the train is traveling at a speed of 50, 60, 70 miles (kilometers) per hour or faster.

Before the turn of the twentieth century, a few physicists began to explore the significance of this strange experience of relative motion. In 1895, for example, Irish physicist George Francis FitzGerald (1851–1901) analyzed the effects of relative motion mathematically and came to a startling conclusion. The length of an object, FitzGerald announced, depended on how fast it was traveling! That is, your trusty meter stick might truly measure 1.000 meter (39.37 inches) when it is at rest. But find a way to get it moving at speeds of a few thousand meters per second, and it will begin to shrink. At some point, it may measure only 0.999 meter, or 0.900 meter, or even 0.500 meter.

Even then, the length of the stick would depend on the person doing the measuring. The shrinkage taking place as the speed of the meter stick increases would be noticeable only to someone at rest compared to the meter stick itself. A person traveling with the meter stick would notice no change at all.

The special theory

The mathematics used by FitzGerald to reach this conclusion is beyond the scope of this book. In fact, the details of all theories of relativity are quite complex, and only some general conclusions can be described here.

Einstein's work on relativity is of primary importance because he was the first physicist to work out in detail all of the implications of the physical properties of moving systems. He began his analysis with only two simple assumptions. First, he assumed that the speed of light is always the same. That is, suppose you could measure the speed of light in your back yard, on a Boeing 747 flying over Detroit, in a rocket ship on its way to the Moon, or on the outer edges of a black hole. No matter where the measurement is made, Einstein said, the speed of light is always the same.

Einstein's second assumption is that the laws of physics are always the same everywhere. Should you someday be able to travel to Mars or to that black hole, you will not have to learn a whole new set of physical laws. They will be the same as those we use here on Earth.

Albert Einstein. *(Reproduced courtesy of the Library of Congress.)*

How did Einstein decide on just these two assumptions and not other possible assumptions? The answer is that he had a hunch—he made a guess as to what he thought would be most basic about anything we could study in the universe. A part of his genius is that his hunches were apparently correct: a whole new kind of physics, relativistic physics, has been built up on them. And the new science seems to work very well, suggesting that its basic assumptions are probably correct.

Conclusions from special relativity. Einstein was a theoretical physicist; he did not spend any time in laboratories trying out his ideas with experiments. Instead, he tried to determine—using logic and mathematics alone—what the consequences would be of his initial assumptions. Eventually he was able to derive mathematical equations that described the physical properties of systems in motion. Some of the conclusions he drew were the following:

1. The length of an object is a function of the speed at which it is traveling. The faster the object travels, the shorter the object becomes.

2. The mass of an object is also a function of the speed at which it is traveling. The faster the object travels, the heavier it becomes.

3. Time slows down as an object increases in speed.

Think for a moment about the logical consequences of just these three points. First, none of the effects is of much practical importance until an object is traveling close to the speed of light. If you tried to detect changes in length, mass, or time in a moving train, you'd have no success at all. It is not until one approaches speeds of about 167,000 miles (270,000 kilometers) per second (about 90 percent the speed of light) that such effects are noticeable.

But what effects they are! An object traveling at the speed of light would have its length reduced to zero, its mass increased to infinity, and the passage of time reduced to zero. Any clocks attached to the object would stop.

Energy and mass

Einstein made one other remarkable discovery in working out the meaning of relativity: he found that the two concepts we think of as energy and mass are really two manifestations of the same phenomenon. This discovery marked a real revolution in thinking. Prior to Einstein's time, scientists thought of mass as being the "stuff" of which objects are made, and they thought of energy as the force that caused matter to move. No one would have imagined that the two had anything at all in common.

What Einstein showed was that it was possible to take a piece of matter and convert it all into energy. Or, by contrast, one could capture a burst of energy and convert it into a piece of matter. He even developed a formula for showing how much mass is equivalent to how much energy: $E = mc^2$, where E is the amount of energy involved, m the amount of mass, and c the velocity of light.

Other implications

The implications of the theory of relativity are unbelievably extensive. Einstein went on to suggest other revolutionary ways of looking at the natural world. For example, scientists had always taken it for granted that the natural world can be described in three dimensions—the three dimensions that we all live in: length, width, and height. All of physics and most of mathematics had traditionally been built on that concept.

Einstein suggested that the world had to be viewed in terms of four dimensions: the three dimensions with which we are familiar and time. That is, if we want to study any object in complete detail, we have to be able to state not only its length, its width, and its height, but also its place on the world's time line. That is, the object is traveling through time as we study it; under many circumstances, changes in its place on the world time line must be taken into consideration.

In addition, Einstein suggested an entirely new way of thinking about space and time. He said that rather than imagining the universe as the inside of an enormous balloon, we should think about it as consisting of curved surfaces over which light and other objects travel.

Tests of relativity

One of the most remarkable things about Einstein's theories is the speed with which they were accepted by other physicists. As revolutionary as his ideas were, physicists quickly saw the logic of Einstein's arguments. Some physicists and many nonscientists, however, wanted to see experimental evidence in the real world that his ideas were correct.

One proof for Einstein's theory is his equation representing the relationship of energy and mass, $E = mc^2$. It is upon this principle that nuclear weapons and nuclear power plants operate.

But other pieces of experimental proof were eventually discovered for Einstein's theories. One of those was obtained in 1919. Einstein had predicted that light will be bent out of a straight path if it passes near to a very massive object. He said that the gravitational field of the object would have an effect on light much as it does on other objects.

An opportunity to test that prediction occurred during a solar eclipse that occurred on May 29, 1919. Astronomers waited until the Sun was completely blocked out during the eclipse, then took a photograph of the stars behind the Sun. They found that the stars appeared to be in a somewhat different position than had been expected. The reason for the apparent displacement of the stars' position was that the light they emitted was bent slightly as it passed the Sun on its way to Earth.

Significance of relativity theory

Einstein's theories have had some practical applications, as demonstrated by the use of $E = mc^2$ in solving problems of nuclear energy. But far more important has been its effect on the way that scientists, and even some nonscientists, view the universe. His theories have changed the way we understand gravity and the universe in general. In that respect, the theories of relativity produced a revolution in physics matched only once or twice in all of previous human history.

[*See also* **Black hole; Light; Nuclear fission; Physics; Pulsar; Quasar; Space; Time**]

Reproduction

A hydra budding. Budding is a form of asexual reproduction, in which a small part of the parent's body separates and develops into a new individual. (Reproduced by permission of Photo Researchers, Inc.)

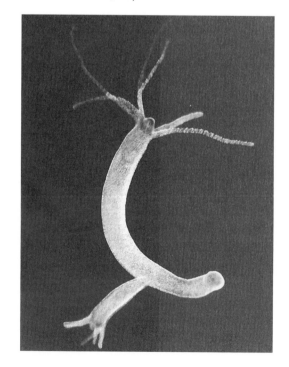

Reproduction is the process by which plants and animals produce offspring. Reproduction may be asexual or sexual. Asexual reproduction occurs when a single cell divides to form two daughter cells that are genetically identical to the parent cell. Sexual reproduction involves the union of an egg (female sex cell) and sperm (male sex cell) to produce a cell that is genetically different than the parent cells.

Asexual reproduction

Asexual reproduction usually occurs by mitosis, a process in which the chromosomes in a cell's nucleus are duplicated before cell division. (Chromosomes are structures that organize genetic information in the nuclei of cells. Genes are units of hereditary information that control what traits are passed from one generation to another.) After the nucleus divides, the cytoplasm of the cell splits, forming two new daughter cells having nuclei with the same number and kind of chromosomes as the parent. Asexual reproduction occurs rapidly and can produce many individuals in a short amount of time. For example, some bacteria that reproduce in this way double their numbers every 20 minutes.

Words to Know

Budding: A form of asexual reproduction in which a small part of the parent's body separates and develops into a new individual.

Chromosome: Structures that organize genetic information in the nuclei of cells.

Cytoplasm: The semifluid substance of a cell containing organelles and enclosed by the cell membrane.

Diploid: Having two sets of chromosomes.

Fragmentation: The regeneration of an entire individual from a broken off piece of an organism.

Gamete: A male or female sex cell.

Gene: A section of a chromosome that carries instructions for the formation, functioning, and transmission of specific traits from one generation to another.

Haploid: Having a single set of unpaired chromosomes.

Meiosis: Process of cell division by which a diploid cell produces four haploid cells.

Mitosis: Process of cell division resulting in the formation of two daughter cells genetically identical to the parent cell.

Zygote: A diploid cell formed by the union of two haploid gametes.

Bacteria, algae, most protozoa, yeast, dandelions, and flatworms all reproduce asexually. Yeasts reproduce asexually by budding, a process in which a small bulge, or bud, forms on the outer edge of a yeast cell and eventually separates, developing into a new cell. Flatworms and starfish can regrow an entire new organism from a piece of their body that is broken off, a process called fragmentation.

Sexual reproduction

In plants and animals, sexual reproduction is the fusion of a sperm and egg, called gametes, from two different parents to form a fertilized egg called a zygote. Gametes are produced in the male testes and female ovaries by a process called meiosis. Meiosis is a type of cell division in which the number of chromosomes in a diploid cell (a cell having two sets of chromosomes in its nucleus) are reduced by half following two successive cell divisions. The four daughter cells that are produced are each haploid, having only half the number of chromosomes as the original diploid cell.

In males, all four daughter cells produced by meiosis become sperm, while in females, only one daughter cell develops into an egg. When an egg and sperm fuse at fertilization, the normal number of chromosomes are restored in the zygote. The shuffling of the parents' genetic material that occurs during meiosis allows for new gene combinations in offspring that over time can improve a species' chances of survival.

Alternation of generations.   Plants go through two stages in their life cycle, called alternation of generations. One is the diploid stage, in which cells undergoing meiosis produce haploid reproductive cells called spores. During the haploid stage, the spores develop into gametophytes (or gamete-producing plants) that produce haploid gametes (eggs and sperm) by mitosis. The gametes unite to produce a diploid zygote that grows into a sporophyte (spore-producing plant), thus completing the cycle.

Hermaphroditism.   Hermaphroditism is a form of sexual reproduction in which an organism has both male and female organs. Thus, hermaph-

Sperm moving over the surface of a uterus. Sexual reproduction involves the union of an egg and sperm to produce a cell that is genetically different than the parent cells. *(Reproduced by permission of Photo Researchers, Inc.)*

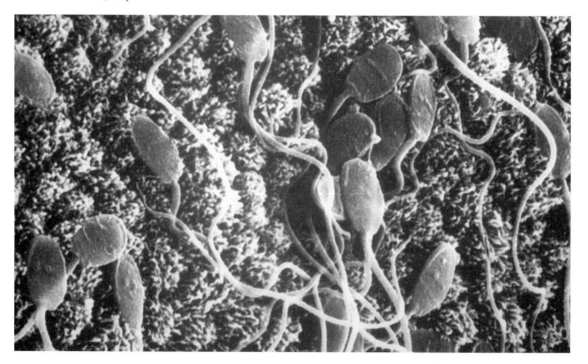

rodites produce both male gametes (sperm) and female gametes (eggs). In some animals, the male and female organs develop at different times. Some hermaphrodites, such as the tapeworm, are capable of fertilizing their own eggs with their own sperm. Most hermaphrodites, however, engage in cross-fertilization, meaning that two organisms of the same species inject sperm into the eggs of the other.

[See also **Chromosome; Nucleic acid**]

Reproductive system

The reproductive system is a group of organized structures that make possible the creation, or reproduction, of new life for continuation of a species. Human reproduction is sexual, meaning that both a male and a female contribute genetic material in the creation of a new individual. During puberty, usually occurring between the ages of nine and fourteen, the reproductive systems of both sexes mature. The ovaries of a female release eggs (female sex cells) and a male's testes produce sperm (male sex cells). Reproduction occurs when a sperm unites with an egg, a process called fertilization.

The male reproductive system

The main tasks of the male reproductive system are to produce sperm cells and to introduce sperm into the female reproductive tract. Sperm are produced in the testes, the pair of male reproductive glands located in the scrotum, a skin-covered sac that hangs from the groin. Within each testis are hollow tubules called seminiferous tubules where sperm cells are produced. The testes also secrete the male hormone testosterone, which stimulates development of the reproductive structures and secondary sexual characteristics (such as deepened voice) at puberty.

After production, sperm cells move to a highly coiled tube called the epididymis, where they mature and are stored. During ejaculation (the ejection of sperm from the penis during orgasm), sperm travel from the epididymis through a long tube called the vas deferens to the urethra. The urethra is a single tube that extends from the bladder to the tip of the penis (and through which urine passes out of the body). Secretions from three different glands mix with sperm before it is ejaculated, forming the seminal fluid, or semen. Ejaculated semen may contain as many as 400 million sperm.

The penis is the male reproductive organ that delivers semen into the female reproductive tract. It consists of a shaft, the glans (or head

Words to Know

Fertilization: The union of an egg and a sperm that initiates the development of a new individual with genetic material from both parents.

Follicle: A sac in the ovary that contains a developing egg surrounded by a group of cells.

Gene: A section of a chromosome that carries instructions for the formation, functioning, and transmission of specific traits from one generation to another.

Hormone: A chemical produced in living cells that is carried by the blood to organs and tissues in distant parts of the body, where it regulates cellular activity.

Menstruation: The monthly shedding of the uterine lining and blood in a nonpregnant female.

Ovary: One of the paired female sex organs that produces eggs and sex hormones.

Ovulation: The release of a mature egg from an ovary.

Ovum: A female sex cell.

Puberty: The period of development of the sexual structures and secondary sexual characteristics in humans and higher primates.

Semen: Fluid containing sperm, nutrients, and mucus that is ejaculated from the penis during orgasm.

Sperm: A male sex cell.

Testis: One of a pair of male sex glands that produces sperm and sex hormones.

region), and a foreskin. It is common practice in certain cultures and religions to have the foreskin removed, or circumcised. During sexual arousal, blood vessels in the tissue of the penis fill with blood, causing it to swell and reach a state of erection. The penis becomes longer, wider, and firm, allowing entry into the female vagina.

The female reproductive system

The main tasks of the female reproductive system are to produce ova, receive sperm from the penis, house and provide nutrients to the

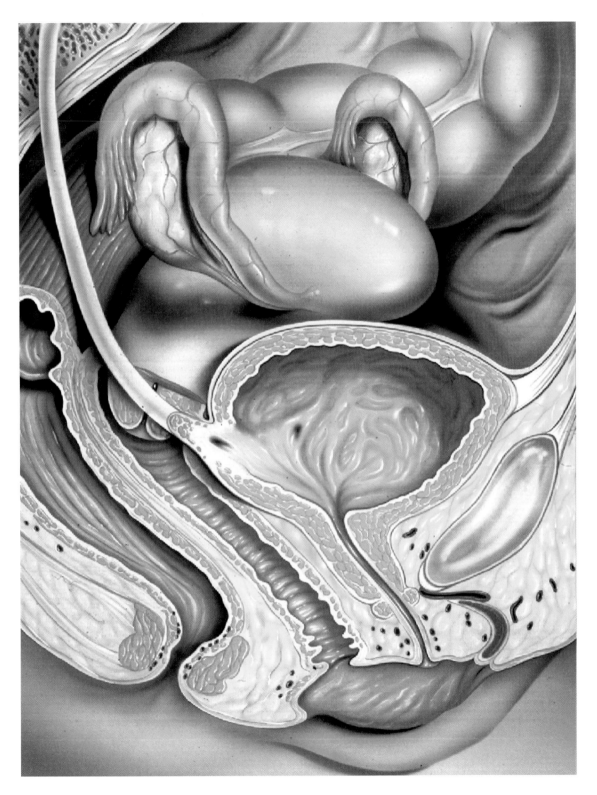

developing embryo (fetus), give birth, and produce milk to feed offspring. Ova are produced in the ovaries, oval-shaped organs in the groin that also produce sex hormones. At birth, a female's ovaries contain hundreds of thousands of undeveloped eggs, each surrounded by a group of cells to form a follicle (sac). However, only about 360 to 480 follicles reach full maturity.

During puberty, the action of hormones cause several follicles to develop each month. Normally, just one follicle fully matures, rupturing and releasing an ovum through the ovary wall in a process called ovulation. The mature egg enters one of the paired fallopian tubes, where it may be fertilized by a sperm and move on to the uterus to develop into a fetus. The lining of the uterus, called the endometrium, prepares for pregnancy each month by becoming thicker. The lining is shed during menstruation if fertilization does not occur.

The uterus, or womb, is the organ in which a fetus develops and receives nutrients and oxygen. At its base lies the cervix, which widens during birth to allow passage of the fetus. The vagina is a muscular tube extending from the uterus to the outside of the body. It is the receptacle for sperm that is ejaculated during sexual intercourse and also forms part of the birth canal. The external genital organs, or vulva, include the labia, clitoris, and mons pubis. The labia are folds of skin on both sides of the openings to the vagina and urethra. The clitoris, a small, sensitive organ located in front of the labia, is comparable to the male penis. The mons pubis is a pad of fatty tissue above the clitoris.

During pregnancy, the female hormones estrogen and progesterone stimulate enlargement of the breasts and mammary glands. About two days after birth, blood levels of these hormones drop, and the pituitary gland releases the hormone prolactin, which stimulates the production of milk. Milk flows through small openings in the nipple of each breast to the nursing infant.

[*See also* **Birth; Contraception; Hormone; Reproduction; Sexually transmitted diseases**]

Reptiles

A reptile is an organism in the kingdom Animalia and the class Reptilia. (Kingdoms are the main divisions into which scientists classify all living things on Earth; kingdoms are further subdivided into phylums [or divisions], classes, and orders.) The reptiles include more than 6,000 species grouped into four orders: the turtles (Chelonia), the snakes and lizards (Squamata), the crocodiles and alligators (Crocodilia), and the tuataras (Sphenodonta), large lizardlike animals found only on islands off the coast of New Zealand.

A number of other reptilian orders are now extinct. These include some of the largest animals ever to occupy the planet. Examples include the fishlike ichthyosaurs, the long-necked plesiosaurs, and the huge flying and gliding pterosaurs. The most famous of the extinct reptilian orders were the dinosaurs, that included immense, ferocious predators such as *Tyrannosaurus rex* and enormously large herbivores (plant-eaters) such as *Apatosaurus.*

The first reptiles known in the fossil record lived about 340 million years ago. The last representatives of the dinosaurs became extinct about 65 million years ago, after being the dominant large animals of Earth for more than 250 million years.

Reptiles are extremely diverse in their form and function. They characteristically have four legs, although some groups such as the snakes have become legless. They usually have a tail and a body covered with protective scales or plates. These scales are dry, not slimy as some people believe, and have developed from the animal's epidermis (skin).

A chuckwalla (*Sauromalus obesus*) at the Arizona Sonora Desert Museum. This iguana basks in the sun during the day to reach its preferred body temperature of 100°F (38°C). *(Reproduced by permission of Field Mark Publications.)*

Reptiles are ectotherms (cold-blooded). This means they warm their bodies by absorbing heat from their environment. Thus, a reptile's body temperature fluctuates with changes in the surrounding temperature. The body temperature of snakes, for example, cools in cold weather and warms up in hot weather. Not surprisingly, external temperature plays a major role in determining the activities of reptiles: they are active when it's warm outside and slow down when its cold.

Reptiles reproduce by internal fertilization. Their eggs (sex cells) have a series of membranes (layers) around the embryo (earliest life-form) that allow the exchange of gases and waste. These eggs, known as amniotic eggs, were an important evolutionary adaptation for conserving moisture and allowed the reptiles to adapt to living on land. Most reptiles are oviparous, meaning they lay eggs in a warm place and the eggs are kept warm until they hatch. Some species are ovoviviparous, meaning the eggs are retained within the female throughout their development so that live young reptiles are born.

Some species of reptiles are dangerous to humans and to animals, including the predatory crocodiles and alligators. Some species of snakes are venomous (poisonous) and may bite people or livestock when threatened. Many species of reptiles are economically important and are hunted as food, for their eggs, or for their skin, which can be manufactured into an attractive leather. Many species are kept as interesting pets or in zoos.

Unfortunately, some people have an unreasonable fear of reptiles that has led to many of them being killed. Additionally many species are endangered because their natural habitats have been taken over for agriculture, forestry, or residential development.

[*See also* **Dinosaurs; Snakes**]

Respiration

The term respiration has two relatively distinct meanings in biology. First, respiration is the process by which an organism takes oxygen into its body and then releases carbon dioxide from its body. In this respect, respiration can be regarded as roughly equivalent to "breathing." In some cases, this meaning of the term is extended to mean the transfer of the oxygen from the lungs to the bloodstream and, eventually, into cells. On the other hand, it may refer to the release of carbon dioxide from cells into the bloodstream and, thence, to the lungs.

Words to Know

Aerobic respiration: Respiration that requires the presence of oxygen.

Anaerobic respiration: Respiration that does not require the presence of oxygen.

ATP (adenosine triphosphate): High-energy molecule that cells use to drive energy-requiring processes such as biosynthesis (the production of chemical compounds), growth, and movement.

Capillaries: Very thin blood vessels that join veins to arteries.

Diffusion: Random movement of molecules that leads to a net movement of molecules from a region of high concentration to a region of low concentration.

Fermentation: A chemical reaction by which carbohydrates, such as sugar, are converted into ethyl alcohol.

Gill: An organ used by some animals for breathing consisting of many specialized tissues with infoldings. It allows the animal to absorb oxygen dissolved in water and expel carbon dioxide to the water.

Glucose: also known as blood sugar, a simple sugar broken down in cells to produce energy.

Glycolysis: A series of chemical reactions that takes place in cells by which glucose is converted into pyruvate.

Hemoglobin: Blood protein that can bind with oxygen.

Lactic acid: Similar to lactate, a chemical compound formed in cells from pyruvate in the absence of oxygen.

Pyruvate: The simpler compound glucose is broken down into during the process of glycolysis.

Trachea: A tube used for breathing.

Second, respiration also refers to the chemical reactions that take place within cells by which food is "burned" and converted into carbon dioxide and water. In this respect, respiration is the reverse of photosynthesis, the chemical change that takes place in plants by which carbon dioxide and water are converted into complex organic compounds. To distinguish from the first meaning of respiration, this "burning" of foods is also referred to as aerobic respiration.

Respiration mechanisms

All animals have some mechanism for removing oxygen from the air and transmitting it into their bloodstreams. The same mechanism is used to expel carbon dioxide from the bloodstream into the surrounding environment. In many cases, a special organ is used, such as lungs, trachea, or gills. In the simplest of animals, oxygen and carbon dioxide are exchanged directly between the organism's bloodstream and the surrounding environment. Following are some of the mechanisms that animals have evolved to solve this problem.

Direct diffusion. In direct diffusion, oxygen passes from the environment through cells on the animal's surface and then into individual cells inside. Sponges, jellyfish, and terrestrial flatworms use this primitive method of respiration. These animals do not have special respiratory organs. Microbes, fungi, and plants all obtain the oxygen they use for cellular respiration by direct diffusion through their surfaces.

Diffusion into blood. In diffusion into the blood, oxygen passes through a moist layer of cells on the body surface. From there, it passes through capillary walls and into the blood stream. Once oxygen is in the blood, it moves throughout the body to different tissues and cells. This method also does not rely upon special respiratory organs and is thus quite primitive. However, it is somewhat more advanced than direct diffusion. Annelids (segmented worms) and amphibians use this method of respiration.

Tracheae. In tracheal respiration, air moves through openings in the body surface called spiracles. It then passes into special breathing tubes called tracheae (singular, trachea) that extend into the body. The tracheae divide into many small branches that are in contact with muscles and organs. In small insects, air moves into the tracheae simply by molecular motion. In large insects, body movements assist tracheal air movement. Insects and terrestrial arthropods (organisms with external skeletons) use this method of respiration.

Gills. Fish and other aquatic animals use gills for respiration. Gills are specialized tissues with many infoldings. Each gill is covered by a thin layer of cells and filled with blood capillaries. These capillaries take up oxygen dissolved in water and expel carbon dioxide dissolved in blood.

Lungs. Lungs are special organs in the body cavity composed of many small chambers filled with blood capillaries. After air enters the lungs, oxygen diffuses into the blood stream through the walls of these capillaries. It then moves from the lung capillaries to the different muscles and organs of the body. Humans and other mammals have lungs in which air moves in and out through the same pathway. In contrast, birds have more specialized lungs that use a mechanism called crosscurrent exchange. Crosscurrent exchange allows air to flow in one direction only, making for more efficient oxygen exchange.

Movement of gases through the body

In direct diffusion and tracheal systems, oxygen and carbon dioxide move back and forth directly between cells and the surrounding environment. In other systems, some mechanism is needed to carry these gases between cells and the outside environment. In animals with lungs or gills, oxygen is absorbed by the bloodstream, converted into an unstable (easily broken down) chemical compound, and then carried to cells. When the compound reaches a cell, it breaks down and releases the oxygen. The oxygen then passes into the cell.

In the reverse process, carbon dioxide is released from a cell into the bloodstream. There the carbon dioxide is used to form another unstable chemical compound, which is carried by the bloodstream back to the gills or lungs. At the end of this journey, the compound breaks down and releases the carbon dioxide to the surrounding environment.

Various animals use different substances to form these unstable compounds. In humans, for example, the substance is a compound known as hemoglobin. In the lungs, hemoglobin reacts with oxygen to form oxyhemoglobin. Oxyhemoglobin travels through the bloodstream to cells, where it breaks down to form hemoglobin and oxygen. The oxygen then passes into cells.

On the return trip, hemoglobin combines with carbon dioxide to form carbaminohemoglobin. In this (and other) forms, carbon dioxide is returned to the surrounding environment.

Animals other than humans use compounds other than hemoglobin for the transport of oxygen and carbon dioxide. Certain kinds of annelids (earthworms, various marine worms, and leeches), for example, contain a green blood protein called chlorocruorin that functions in the same way that hemoglobin does in humans.

Whatever substance is used, the compound it forms with oxygen and carbon dioxide must be unstable, it must break down easily. This property is essential if the oxygen and carbon dioxide are to be released easily at the end of their journeys into and out of cells, lungs, and gills.

Cellular respiration. Cellular respiration is a process by which the simple sugar glucose is oxidized (combined with oxygen) to form the energy-rich compound adenosine triphosphate (ATP). Glucose is produced in cells by the breakdown of more complex carbohydrates, including starch, cellulose, and complex sugars such as sucrose (cane or beet sugar) and fructose (fruit sugar). ATP is the compound used by cells to carry out most of their ordinary functions, such as production of new cell parts and chemicals, movement of compounds through cells and the body as a whole, and growth.

The overall chemical change that occurs in cellular respiration can be represented by a fairly simple chemical equation:

$$6C_6H_{12}O_6 + 6\ O_2 \rightarrow 6\ CO_2 + 6\ H_2O + 36\ ATP$$

That equation says that six molecules of glucose ($C_6H_{12}O_6$) react with six molecules of oxygen (O_2) to form six molecules of carbon dioxide (CO_2), six molecules of water (H_2O) and 36 molecules of ATP.

Cellular respiration is, however, a great deal more complicated that this equation would suggest. In fact, nearly two dozen separate chemical reactions are involved in the overall conversion of glucose to carbon dioxide, water, and ATP. Those two dozens reactions can be grouped together into three major cycles: glycolysis, the citric acid (or Krebs) cycle, and the electron transport chain.

In glycolysis, glucose is broken down into a simpler compound known as pyruvate. Pyruvate, in turn, is converted in the citric acid cycle to a variety of energy-rich compounds, such as ATP and NADH (nicotinamide adenine dinucleotide). Finally, all of these energy-rich compounds are converted in the electron transport chain to ATP.

Anaerobic respiration. As the equation above indicates, cellular respiration usually requires the presence of oxygen and is, therefore, often known as aerobic (or "using oxygen") respiration. Another form of respiration is possible, one that does not make use of oxygen. That form of respiration is known as anaerobic (or "without oxygen") respiration.

Anaerobic respiration begins, as does aerobic respiration, with glycolysis. In the next step, however, pyruvate is not passed onto the citric acid cycle. Instead, it undergoes one of two other chemical reactions. In the first of these reactions, the pyruvate is converted to ethyl alcohol in a process known as fermentation. Fermentation is a well-known chemical reaction by which grapes, barley, rice, and other grains are used to make wine, beer, and other alcoholic beverages.

The second anaerobic reaction occurs when cells are unable to obtain oxygen by methods they normally use. For example, a person who exercises vigorously may not be able to inhale oxygen fast enough to meet the needs of his or her cells. (Glucose is used up faster than oxygen is supplied to the cells.) In that case, cells switch over to anaerobic respiration. They convert glucose to pyruvate and then to another chemical known as lactate or lactic acid (two forms of the same compound). As lactic acid begins to build up in cells, it causes an irritation similar to placing vinegar (acetic acid) in an open wound.

Most cells are able to switch from aerobic to anaerobic respiration when necessary. But they are generally not able to continue producing energy by this process for very long.

Scientists believe that the first organisms to appear on Earth's surface were anaerobic organisms. Those organisms arose when Earth's atmosphere contained very little oxygen. They had to produce the energy they needed, therefore, by mechanisms that did not require oxygen. As the composition of Earth's atmosphere changed to include more oxygen, organisms evolved to adapt to that condition.

[*See also* **Bacteria; Blood; Diffusion; Fermentation; Metabolism; Oxygen family; Respiratory system; Yeast**]

Respiratory system

Respiration is the process by which living organisms take in oxygen and release carbon dioxide. The human respiratory system, working in conjunction with the circulatory system, supplies oxygen to the body's cells, removing carbon dioxide in the process. The exchange of these gases occurs across cell membranes both in the lungs (external respiration) and in the body tissues (internal respiration). Breathing, or pulmonary ventilation, describes the process of inhaling and exhaling air. The human respiratory system consists of the respiratory tract and the lungs.

Respiratory tract

The respiratory tract cleans, warms, and moistens air during its trip to the lungs. The tract can be divided into an upper and a lower part. The upper part consists of the nose, nasal cavity, pharynx (throat), and larynx (voice box). The lower part consists of the trachea (windpipe), bronchi, and bronchial tree.

The nose has openings to the outside that allow air to enter. Hairs inside the nose trap dirt and keep it out of the respiratory tract. The

Words to Know

Alveoli: Tiny air-filled sacs in the lungs where the exchange of oxygen and carbon dioxide occurs between the lungs and the bloodstream.

Bronchi: Two main branches of the trachea leading into the lungs.

Bronchial tree: Branching, air-conducting subdivisions of the bronchi in the lungs.

Diaphragm: Dome-shaped sheet of muscle located below the lungs separating the thoracic and abdominal cavities that contracts and expands to force air in and out of the lungs.

Epiglottis: Flap of elastic cartilage covering the larynx that allows air to pass through the trachea while keeping solid particles and liquids out.

Pleura: Membranous sac that envelops each lung and lines the thoracic cavity.

external nose leads to a large cavity within the skull, the nasal cavity. This cavity is lined with mucous membrane and fine hairs called cilia. Mucus moistens the incoming air and traps dust. The cilia move pieces of the mucus with its trapped particles to the throat, where it is spit out or swallowed. Stomach acids destroy bacteria in swallowed mucus. Blood vessels in the nose and nasal cavity release heat and warm the entering air.

Air leaves the nasal cavity and enters the pharynx. From there it passes into the larynx, which is supported by a framework of cartilage (tough, white connective tissue). The larynx is covered by the epiglottis, a flap of elastic cartilage that moves up and down like a trap door. The epiglottis stays open during breathing, but closes during swallowing. This valve mechanism keeps solid particles (food) and liquids out of the trachea. If something other than air enters the trachea, it is expelled through automatic coughing.

Air enters the trachea in the neck. Mucous membrane lines the trachea and C-shaped cartilage rings reinforce its walls. Elastic fibers in the trachea walls allow the airways to expand and contract during breathing, while the cartilage rings prevent them from collapsing. The trachea divides behind the sternum (breastbone) to form a left and right branch, called bronchi (pronounced BRONG-key), each entering a lung.

The lungs

The lungs are two cone-shaped organs located in the chest or thoracic cavity. The heart separates them. The right lung is somewhat larger than the left. A sac, called the pleura, surrounds and protects the lungs. One layer of the pleura attaches to the wall of the thoracic cavity and the other layer encloses the lungs. A fluid between the two membrane layers reduces friction and allows smooth movement of the lungs during breathing.

The lungs are divided into lobes, each one of which receives its own bronchial branch. Inside the lungs, the bronchi subdivide repeatedly into smaller airways. Eventually they form tiny branches called terminal

The human respiratory sys-tem. *(Reproduced by permis-sion of The Gale Group.)*

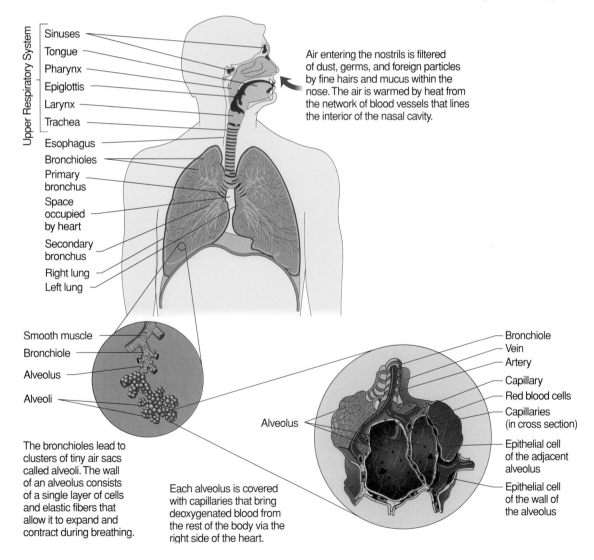

Upper Respiratory System

- Sinuses
- Tongue
- Pharynx
- Epiglottis
- Larynx
- Trachea
- Esophagus
- Bronchioles
- Primary bronchus
- Space occupied by heart
- Secondary bronchus
- Right lung
- Left lung

Air entering the nostrils is filtered of dust, germs, and foreign particles by fine hairs and mucus within the nose. The air is warmed by heat from the network of blood vessels that lines the interior of the nasal cavity.

- Smooth muscle
- Bronchiole
- Alveolus
- Alveoli

The bronchioles lead to clusters of tiny air sacs called alveoli. The wall of an alveolus consists of a single layer of cells and elastic fibers that allow it to expand and contract during breathing.

- Alveolus

Each alveolus is covered with capillaries that bring deoxygenated blood from the rest of the body via the right side of the heart.

- Bronchiole
- Vein
- Artery
- Capillary
- Red blood cells
- Capillaries (in cross section)
- Epithelial cell of the adjacent alveolus
- Epithelial cell of the wall of the alveolus

bronchioles. Terminal bronchioles have a diameter of about 0.02 inch (0.5 millimeter). This branching network within the lungs is called the bronchial tree.

The terminal bronchioles enter cup-shaped air sacs called alveoli (pronounced al-VEE-o-leye). The average person has a total of about 700 million gas-filled alveoli in the lungs. These provide an enormous surface area for gas exchange. A network of capillaries (tiny blood vessels) surrounds each alveoli. As blood passes through these vessels and air fills the alveoli, the exchange of gases takes place: oxygen passes from the alveoli into the capillaries while carbon dioxide passes from the capillaries into the alveoli.

This process—external respiration—causes the blood to leave the lungs laden with oxygen and cleared of carbon dioxide. When this blood reaches the cells of the body, internal respiration takes place. The oxygen diffuses or passes into the tissue fluid, and then into the cells. At the same time, carbon dioxide in the cells diffuses into the tissue fluid and then into the capillaries. The carbon dioxide-filled blood then returns to the lungs for another cycle.

Breathing

Breathing exchanges gases between the outside air and the alveoli of the lungs. Lung expansion is brought about by two important muscles, the diaphragm (pronounced DIE-a-fram) and the intercostal muscles. The diaphragm is a dome-shaped sheet of muscle located below the lungs that separates the thoracic and abdominal cavities. The intercostal muscles are located between the ribs.

Nerves from the brain send impulses to the diaphragm and intercostal muscles, stimulating them to contract or relax. When the diaphragm contracts, it moves down. The dome is flattened, and the size of the chest cavity is increased. When the intercostal muscles contract, the ribs move up and outward, which also increases the size of the chest cavity. By contracting, the diaphragm and intercostal muscles reduce the pressure inside the lungs relative to the pressure of the outside air. As a consequence, air rushes into the lungs during inhalation. During exhalation, the reverse occurs. The diaphragm relaxes and its dome curves up into the chest cavity, while the intercostal muscles relax and bring the ribs down and inward. The diminished size of the chest cavity increases the pressure in the lungs, thereby forcing air out.

A healthy adult breathes in and out about 12 times per minute, but this rate changes with exercise and other factors. Total lung capacity is about 12.5 pints (6 liters). Under normal circumstances, humans inhale and exhale about one pint (475 milliliters) of air in each cycle. Only about three-quarters of this air reaches the alveoli. The rest of the air remains in the respiratory tract. Regardless of the volume of air breathed in and out, the lungs always retain about 2.5 pints (1200 milliliters) of air. This residual air keeps the alveoli and bronchioles partially filled at all times.

Respiratory disorders

The respiratory system is open to airborne microorganisms and outside pollution. Some respiratory disorders are relatively mild and, unfortunately, very familiar. Excess mucus, coughing, and sneezing are all symptoms of the common cold, which is an inflammation of the mucous membrane lining the nose and nasal cavity. Viruses, bacteria, and allergens are among the causes of the common cold.

Since the respiratory lining is continuous, nasal cavity infections often spread. Laryngitis, an inflammation of the vocal cords, results in hoarseness and loss of voice. Viruses, irritating chemicals in the air, and overuse of the voice are causes of laryngitis.

Pneumonia, inflammation of the alveoli, is most commonly caused by bacteria and viruses. During a bout of pneumonia, the inflamed alveoli fill up with fluid and dead bacteria (pus). Breathing becomes difficult. Patients come down with fever, chills, and pain, coughing up phlegm and sometimes blood.

Sufferers of bronchitis, an inflammation of the bronchi, also cough up thick phlegm. There are two types of bronchitis, acute and chronic. Acute bronchitis can be a complication of a cold or flu. Bacteria, smoking, and air pollution can also cause acute bronchitis. This type of bronchitis clears up in a short time. Chronic bronchitis is a long-term illness that is mainly caused by air pollution and tobacco smoke. There is a persistent cough and congestion of the airways.

In emphysema, also caused by smoking, the walls of the alveoli disintegrate and the alveoli blend together. They form large air pockets from which air cannot escape. This cuts down the surface area for gas exchange. It becomes difficult for the patient to exhale. The extra work of exhaling over several years can cause the chest to enlarge and become barrel-shaped. The body is unable to repair the damage to the lungs, and the disease can lead to respiratory failure.

Asthma is a disorder of the nervous system. While the cause for the condition is unknown, it is known that allergies can trigger an asthma attack. Nerve messages cause extreme muscle spasms in the lungs that either narrow or close the bronchioles. A tightness is felt in the chest and breathing becomes difficult. Asthma attacks come and go in irregular patterns, and they vary in degree of severity.

Lung cancer is the leading cause of cancer death in men. It is the second leading cause of cancer death (after breast cancer) in women. Cigarette smoking is the main cause of lung cancer. Air pollution, radioactive minerals, and asbestos also cause lung cancer. The symptoms of the disease include a chronic cough from bronchitis, coughing up blood, short-

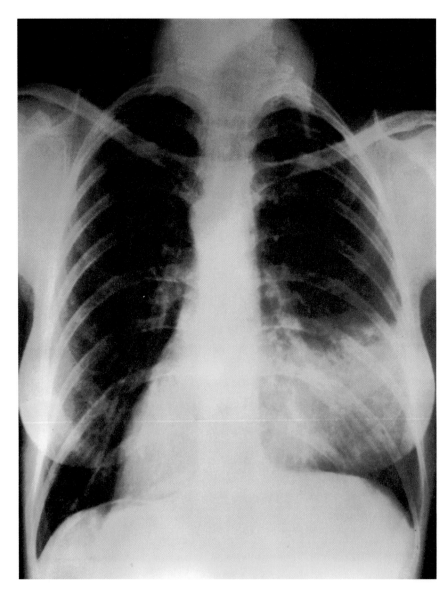

A chest X ray showing pneumonia in the lower lobe of the patient's right lung. With pneumonia, the alveoli of the lungs become blocked with fluid and dead bacteria. (Reproduced by permission of Photo Researchers, Inc.)

ness of breath, and chest pain. Lung cancer can spread in the lung area. Unchecked, it can spread to other parts of the body.

[*See also* **Blood**]

Rh factor

Rh factor is a protein called an antigen that is found on the red blood cells of most people. (An antigen is any substance that the body considers "foreign" and thus stimulates the body to produce antibodies against it.) Rh factor, like the blood types A, B, and O, is inherited from one's parents. A simple blood test can determine blood type, including the presence of the Rh factor. About 85 percent of white Americans and 95 percent of African Americans have the Rh factor and are known as Rh-positive. Those without the Rh factor are Rh-negative.

Rh factor in pregnancy

Rh factor plays a critical role in some pregnancies. If a woman who is Rh-negative becomes pregnant by a man who is Rh- positive, the fetus may inherit the Rh factor from its father and be Rh-positive. If the blood of the fetus becomes mixed with the mother's Rh-negative blood, a disease called erythroblastosis fetalis can occur in future pregnancies, resulting in destruction of the fetus's red blood cells, brain damage, and even death.

The mixing of blood does not normally occur but may take place before or during birth if a tear in the placenta (the organ through which nutrients pass from the mother to the fetus) allows some fetal blood to enter the mother's circulatory system. If this happens, the fetus's red blood cells bearing the Rh factor stimulate the mother's white blood cells to produce antibodies against the foreign antigen. The mother's blood is now sensitized to the Rh factor.

Once a mother's blood is sensitized, the antibodies her body produces in response to the Rh antigen can cross the placenta and attach to the red blood cells of any Rh-positive fetus that she carries. This results in the rupture of the fetus's red blood cells, causing anemia (a condition marked by weakness and fatigue due to a reduced number of red blood cells). Severe anemia can lead to heart failure and death. The breakdown of red blood cells also causes the overproduction of a reddish-yellow substance called bilirubin. An infant with high levels of bilirubin will develop jaundice (have a yellowish appearance) and may suffer brain damage.

Prevention of erythroblastosis fetalis

Erythroblastosis fetalis can be prevented by administering a preparation of anti-Rh factor antibodies to an Rh-negative mother whose blood has not yet produced antibodies to the Rh antigen. The preparation, known as Rh immune globulin, rids the mother's blood of fetal red blood cells before she can become sensitized to them. Rh immune globulin is given whenever there is a possibility of fetal blood mixing with maternal blood, such as following childbirth, an abortion, a miscarriage, or prenatal testing.

Treatment for erythroblastosis fetalis

Treatment for erythroblastosis fetalis depends to what extent the fetus is affected by the action of its mother's anti-Rh-factor antibodies. A fetus whose red blood cells are being severely destroyed can be treated

The path of Rh disease.
(Reproduced by permission of The Gale Group.)

A reduction in red blood cells leads to anemia, a condition marked by weakness and fatigue. Severe anemia can lead to heart failure and death. The breakdown of red blood cells also causes the formation of bilirubin, the build up of which can lead to jaundice and possibly brain damage.

An Rh positive father and Rh negative mother may conceive an Rh positive baby.

In a subsequent pregnancy with an Rh positive baby there is the risk that it will develop Rh disease. Even though the blood circulation of the mother is separate from that of the child, the antibodies in her system can cross the placenta, enter the bloodstream of the baby, and cause its red blood cells to be killed.

This usually isn't a problem if it's the mother's first pregnancy with an Rh positive child, because her blood circulation is separate from that of the baby.

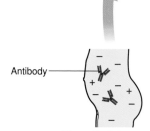

Antibody

The mother's immune system recognizes the cells as foreign and develops antibodies against them.

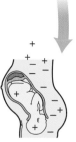

At birth, or after an abortion or miscarriage, Rh positive blood cells from the baby enter the mother's bloodstream.

Words to Know

Antibody: A protein produced by certain cells of the body as an immune (disease-fighting) response to a specific foreign antigen.

Antigen: Any substance that the body considers foreign and that stimulates the body to produce antibodies against it.

Bilirubin: Reddish-yellow substance produced by the breakdown of red blood cells.

Erythroblastosis fetalis: A disease of fetuses and newborns caused by the mixing of fetal Rh-positive blood with maternal Rh-negative blood and resulting in rupture of fetal red blood cells.

Placenta: The organ formed during pregnancy in mammals through which substances are exchanged between mother and fetus.

Protein: Large molecules that are essential to the structure and functioning of all living cells.

Sensitization: The initial exposure to a specific antigen that causes an immune reaction in the body.

with transfusions (replacement) of Rh-negative blood while it is still in the uterus. If the fetus shows signs of illness close to its anticipated birth, the physician may elect to deliver the baby early. The baby's blood is then replaced with Rh-negative blood following birth.

A pregnant woman who is already sensitized to the Rh antigen can have her doctor carefully monitor the level of antibodies in her blood throughout her pregnancy. If the levels rise, the fetus will need special attention. Unfortunately, once a woman is sensitized, she will always produce antibodies when exposed to the Rh antigen.

[*See also* **Antibody and antigen; Blood**]

River

A river is a natural stream of freshwater that is larger than a brook or creek. Rivers are normally the main channels or largest tributaries of drainage systems. Typical rivers begin with a flow from headwater areas made up

Words to Know

Brook: A significant, continuously flowing body of water formed by the convergence of a number of rills.

Catchment area: Also known as a drainage basin, the entire land area drained by a river.

Episodic rivers: Rarely occurring rivers formed from runoff channels in very dry regions.

Perennial rivers: Rivers that have a constant stream-flow throughout the year, usually located in more humid climates where rainfall exceeds evaporation rates.

Periodic rivers: Rivers that run dry on occasion, usually located in arid climates where evaporation is greater than precipitation.

Rill: A small brook that forms from surface runoff.

Runnels: Eroded shallow channels created when rills pass over fine soil.

Tributary: A stream or other body of water that flows into a larger one.

Watershed: A ridge of high land that separates the catchment area of one river system from that of another; also used synonymously with catchment area.

of small tributaries, such as springs. They then travel in meandering paths at various speeds. Finally, they discharge or flow out into desert basins, into major lakes, or most likely, into oceans.

Sixteen of Earth's largest rivers account for close to one-half of the planet's river flow. The world's longest river is the Nile River in Africa, which runs 4,187 miles (6,739 kilometers) from its source in Burundi to the Mediterranean Sea. However, the world's largest river is the Amazon River in South America. It runs about 3,900 miles (6,275 kilometers) from its source in the Andes Mountains in Peru to the southern Atlantic Ocean. Discharging an average of 7,000,000 cubic feet (198,000 cubic meters) of water each second, the Amazon River alone accounts for 20 percent of the water discharged each year by Earth's rivers.

Formation of rivers

Every river has a point of origin. Because gravity plays a key role in the direction that rivers take, rivers almost always follow a downhill slope. Thus, the point of origin for rivers tends to be the highest point in the watercourse. Some rivers start from springs, especially in humid climates. Springs occur as groundwater rises to Earth's surface and flows away. Other rivers originate from lakes, marshes, or runoff from melting glaciers located high in the mountains. Often, rivers having their beginnings in huge glaciers are quite large by the time they emerge from openings in the ice.

Precipitation, such as rainwater or snow, on highlands is the source of the water for most rivers. When a heavy rain falls on ground that is steeply sloped or is already saturated with water, water runoff trickles down Earth's surface rather than being absorbed. Initially, the water runs in an evenly distributed, paper-thin sheet, called surface runoff. After it travels a short distance, the water begins to run in small parallel rivulets called rills. At the same time, the water becomes turbulent. As these rills pass over fine soil or silt, they begin to dig shallow channels, called runnels. This is the first stage of erosion.

The Parana River in Brazil. *(Reproduced by permission of Photo Researchers, Inc.)*

These parallel rills do not last very long, perhaps only a few yards. Fairly soon, the rills unite with one another until enough of them merge to form a stream. After a number of rills converge, the resulting stream is a significant, continuously flowing body of water, called a brook. As a brook flows along and groundwater supplies add to the amount of water the brook carries, it soon becomes a river.

River systems

Rivers can have different origins and, as they travel, often merge with other bodies of water. Thus, the complete river system consists of not only the river itself but also all of its converging tributaries. As rivers make the trip from their source to their eventual destination, the larger ones tend to meet and merge with other rivers. Resembling the trunk and branches of a tree, the water flowing in the main stream often meets the water from its tributaries at sharp angles, combining to form the river system. As long as there are no major areas of seepage and the evaporation level remains normal, the volume of water carried by a river increases from its source to its mouth with every tributary.

Along its path, a single river obtains water from surface runoff from different sections of land. The area from which a particular river obtains its water is defined as its catchment area (sometimes called a drainage basin). The high ground or divide separating different catchment areas is called a watershed. At every point along the line of a watershed, there is a downward slope going into the middle of the catchment area (watershed is also often used as a synonym for catchment area).

Climactic influences

Climate conditions and rainfall patterns have a great effect on rivers, dividing them into three general types. The first are the perennial or permanent rivers. Normally, these rivers are located in more humid climates where rainfall exceeds evaporation rates. Although these rivers may experience seasonal fluctuations in their water levels, they have constant stream-flow throughout the year. With few exceptions, stream-flow in these rivers increases downstream, and these rivers empty into larger bodies of water such as oceans. In fact, 68 percent of rivers drain into oceans. All of the world's major rivers are perennial rivers.

The second type are the periodic rivers. These rivers are characterized by an intermittent (not continuous) stream-flow. Usually appearing in arid climates where evaporation is greater than precipitation, these rivers are dry on occasion. Typically, these rivers have a decrease in stream-flow as they travel. Often, they do not reach the sea, but instead run into an inland drainage basin.

The third type are the episodic rivers. These rivers are actually the runoff channels of very dry regions. Where there is only a slight amount of rainfall, it often evaporates quickly. Thus, this type of stream-flow occurs rarely.

Human control of rivers

For centuries, rivers have been very important to human society. Rivers have provided vital transportation links between oceans and inland areas, and have also provided water for drinking, washing, and irrigation. The need to prevent natural flooding and the desire to utilize the rich soil of flood plains for farming have made river management a key part of civil engineering.

While the techniques of river management are fairly well understood, true river management is not commonly put into practice because

The Susquehanna River at 10 to 17 feet (3 to 5 meters) above flood levels near Wilkes-Barre, Pennsylvania, after Tropical Storm Agnes dropped record rainfalls. *(Reproduced by permission of the U.S. Coast Guard.)*

of the expense and the size of the projects. In fact, none of the major rivers in the world is controlled or even managed in a way that modern engineering and biological techniques would allow. So far, only medium-sized streams have been successfully managed.

[*See also* **Dams; Hydrologic cycle; Lake; Water**]

Robotics

Robotics is the science of designing and building machines (robots) that are directed by computers to perform tasks traditionally carried out by humans. The word robot comes from a play written in 1920 by the Czech author Karel Capek. Capek's *R.U.R.* (for Rossum's Universal Robots) is the story of an inventor who creates humanlike machines designed to take over many forms of human work.

Historical background

The origin of robotics can be traced back to early Egypt, where priests used steam-activated mechanisms to open temple doors. This action helped convince their followers of their "mystical" powers. Ancient Greeks, Chinese, and Ethiopians also experimented with steam-powered devices.

In the late 1700s, Swiss brothers Pierre and Henri Jacquet-Droz created *Jacquemarts,* spring-powered mannequins that could play musical instruments, draw pictures, write, and strike the hours on clock bells.

In 1892, Seward Babbitt invented the motorized crane that could reach into a furnace, grasp a hot ingot of steel, and place it where directed. Although none of these devises were true robots as we known them today, they represent the first steps of automation and robotics technology.

Robots at work: The present day

Robots have come to play a widespread and crucial role in many industrial operations today. The work that robots do can be classified into three major categories: the assembly and finishing of products; the movement of materials and objects; and the performance of work in environmentally difficult or hazardous situations.

Assembly and finishing of products.   The most common single application of robots is in welding. About one-quarter of all robots used by industry have this function. Welding robots can have a variety of appearances, but they tend to consist of one large arm that can rotate in various directions. At the end of the arm is a welding gun that actually forms the weld between two pieces of metal.

Closely related types of work now done by robots include cutting, grinding, polishing, drilling, sanding, painting, spraying, and otherwise treating the surface of a product. As with welding, activities of this kind are usually performed by one-armed robots that hang from the ceiling, project outward from a platform, or reach into a product from some other angle.

Another example in which robots have replaced humans in industrial operations is on the assembly line. In many industrial plants today, the assembly line of humans has been replaced by an assembly line of robots that does the same job, but more safely and more efficiently.

Movement of materials. Many industrial operations involve the lifting and moving of large, heavy objects over and over again. One way to perform these operations is with heavy machinery operated by human workers. But another method that is more efficient and safer is to substitute robots for the human-operated machinery.

An experimental type of heavy-duty robot is an exoskeleton—a metallic contraption that surrounds a human worker. The human can step inside the exoskeleton, placing his or her arms and legs into the corre-

A police robot handling a live bomb by remote control. *(Reproduced by permission of Photo Researchers, Inc.)*

sponding limbs of the exoskeleton. By operating the exoskeleton's controls, the human can magnify his or her strength many times, picking up and handling objects that would otherwise be much too heavy to lift.

Hazardous or remote-duty robots. Robots are commonly used in places where humans can go only at risk to their own health or where they cannot go at all. Industries where nuclear materials are used often make use of robots so that human workers are not exposed to the dangerous effects of radiation.

Robots have also been useful in space research. In 1976, the space probes *Viking 1* and *Viking 2* landed on the planet Mars. These two probes were some of the most complex and sophisticated robots ever built. Their job was to analyze the planet's surface. They did so by using a long arm to dig into the ground and take out samples of Martian soil. The soil samples were then transported to one of three chemical laboratories within the robot, where the soil underwent automated chemical analysis. The results of these analyses were then transmitted to receiving stations on Earth.

How more complex robots work

Sophisticated robots are able to imitate some of the actions of humans because of three key components. First, they are able to respond to changes in the world around them by using visual or tactile (touch) sensors to obtain information. Second, they have a set of instructions (a program) implanted in their computer-brain giving them a core base of knowledge. Third, they are able to combine information from their senses with that in their computer-brain to make decisions and perform actions.

Robots of the future?

In early 2001, scientists at a U.S. government national security laboratory provided a glimpse of the possible future of robots when they showed off what is perhaps the world's smallest robot. The diminutive robot weighs less than 1 ounce (28 grams) and is 0.25 cubic inch (4 cubic centimeters) in size. It can stop and almost sit on a dime. It sports track wheels similar to those on a tank and has an 8K ROM processor. The robot can be equipped with a camera, microphone, and a chemical micro-sensor, and in the future it may carry a miniature video camera and infrared or radio wireless two-way communications equipment. Scientist hope the robot (and others like it) may someday be used to perform a host of arduous tasks like disabling land mines or searching for lost humans. It could even be used in intelligence gathering.

[*See also* **Artificial intelligence; Automation**]

Rockets and missiles

The term rocket is used in two different ways: (1) it is used to describe a jet engine that does not depend on air for its operation but instead carries its own fuel and oxidizing agent, and (2) it is used to describe any vehicle that is powered by a rocket engine.

For example, a fireworks device is a kind of rocket engine. It contains the fuel and oxidizing agent needed to put it into the air as well as the chemicals needed to give the colored display typical of fireworks. A rocket fired to the Moon illustrates both meanings of the term. The vehicle itself carries a rocket engine as well as living quarters for humans, equipment for experiments, instruments needed for communication, and other units. The rocket in this case is both the engine that propels the vehicle and the vehicle itself.

A missile is an unmanned vehicle propelled through space, usually carrying some type of explosive device intended to do harm to an enemy. A missile, like a rocket, usually carries its own means of propulsion. It may also carry its own guidance system or, alternatively, it may be guided by a ground-based command center.

Rockets have two primary functions. First, they are used to carry out research on Earth's atmosphere, other parts of the solar system, and outer space. Rockets designed to carry instruments no farther than the upper levels of the atmosphere are known as sounding rockets. Those designed to lift spacecraft into orbit or into outer space are known as boosters or as carrier vehicles.

The second function of rockets is use as components of missiles. A large fraction of the research and development on modern rocketry systems has been carried out by or supervised by the military services.

How rockets work

The operation of a rocket is based on Newton's third law of motion. According to that law, every action is accompanied by an equal and opposite reaction. An interesting illustration of this law is the method by which a squid propels itself through the water. The body of the squid contains a sac that holds a dark, watery fluid. When the squid finds it necessary to move, it contracts the sac and expels some of the fluid from an opening in the back of its body. In this example, the expulsion of the watery fluid in a backward direction can be thought of as an action. The equal and opposite reaction that occurs to balance that action is the movement of the squid's body in a forward direction.

↓ Words to Know

Ballistic missile: A missile that travels at a velocity less than that needed to place it in orbit and that, therefore, follows a trajectory (a curved path) back to Earth's surface.

Binder: A material used to hold the fuel and oxidizer together in a solid-fuel rocket.

Booster rocket: A rocket designed to lift a spacecraft into orbit or into outer space.

Carrier vehicle: Another name for a booster rocket.

Grain: The fuel in a solid propellant.

Liquid-fuel rocket: A rocket in which both fuel and oxidizer are in the liquid state.

Plasma: A mass of very hot charged particles.

Solid-fuel rocket: A rocket in which both fuel and oxidizer are in the solid state.

Sounding rockets: Rockets designed to travel no farther than the upper levels of Earth's atmosphere.

A rocket is propelled in a forward direction when, like the squid, a fluid is expelled from the back of its body. In the most common type of rocket, the expelled fluid is a mass of hot gases produced by a chemical reaction inside the body of the rocket. In other types of rockets, the expelled fluid may be a stream of charged particles, or plasma, produced by an electrical, nuclear, or solar process.

Liquid-fuel rockets

Chemical rockets are of two primary types: those that use liquid fuels and those that use solid fuels. The most familiar type of liquid rocket is one in which liquid oxygen is used to oxidize liquid hydrogen. In this reaction, water vapor at very high temperatures (about 2700°C, or 4,900°F) is produced. The water vapor is expelled from the rear of the rocket, pushing the rocket itself forward.

The liquid oxygen/hydrogen rocket requires an external source of energy, such as an electric spark, to initiate the chemical reaction. Some combinations of fuel and oxidizer, however, ignite as soon as they are brought into contact. An example is the liquid combination of nitrogen tetroxide and monomethylhydrazine. These two compounds react with each other spontaneously to produce a temperature of about 2,900°C (5,200°F).

A third type of liquid rocket uses only a single compound. That compound decomposes, producing gases that propel the rocket. An example is hydrogen peroxide. When hydrogen peroxide decomposes, it produces oxygen and water vapor at temperatures of about 745°C (1,370°F) that are ejected from the back of the rocket.

Robert H. Goddard beside
the first rocket to success-
fully use liquid fuel. It flew
on March 16, 1926, at
Auburn, Massachusetts.
*(Reproduced by permission of
National Aeronautics and
Space Administration.)*

Advantages and disadvantages of liquid rockets. Liquid-fuel rockets have a number of advantages. First, they can be turned on and off rather simply (at least in concept) by opening and closing the valves that feed the two components to each other. Also, they tend to provide more power than do solid rockets. Finally, when problems develop in a liquid-fuel rocket, they tend to be less serious than those in a solid-fuel rocket.

However, liquid-fuel rockets also have a number of serious disadvantages. One is that the liquid components often require very special care. Also, liquid fuels must be added to a rocket just before its actual ignition since the components cannot be stored in the rocket body for long periods of time. Finally, the mechanical demands needed for the proper operation of a liquid-fuel system can be very complex and, therefore, subject to a number of possible failures.

Solid-fuel rockets

In a solid-fuel rocket, the fuel and oxidizer exist in the solid, rather than the liquid, state. The combination of fuel and oxidizer, along with a binder to hold them together, is called the grain. The grain usually has a claylike texture. When ignition occurs, the oxidizer reacts with the fuel to produce hot gases that propel the rocket in the same way as with liquid rockets.

Many combinations of materials have been used for the grain in a solid-fuel rocket. One common mixture consists of powdered aluminum metal as the fuel and ammonium perchlorate or ammonium nitrate as the oxidizer. The flame produced by the reaction between these two substances has a temperature of at least 3,000°C (5,400°F). Nitroglycerine in combination with easily oxidizable organic compounds is also widely used. Such combinations have flame temperatures of about 2,250°C (4,100°F).

Advantages and disadvantages of solid fuel rockets. Like liquid-fuel rockets, solid-fuel rockets have both advantages and disadvantages. A solid-fuel rocket can be fueled a long time in advance of a launch without much danger of the fuel's deteriorating or damaging the rocket body. The construction of the rocket body needed to accommodate the solid fuel is also much simpler than that needed for a liquid-fuel rocket. Finally, the fuels themselves in a solid-fuel rocket tend to be safer and easier to work with than those in a liquid-fuel rocket.

Still, solid-fuel rockets have their own drawbacks. Once the fuel in a solid-fuel rocket begins to burn, there is no way to slow it down or turn it off. That means that some of the most serious accidents that can occur with a rocket are those that involve solid-fuel combustion that gets out of control.

Nonchemical rockets

Rockets that operate with solid and liquid chemicals are the only kinds currently in use. Because both kinds of rockets have their own disadvantages, engineers have long explored the possibility of developing other rocket types. As early as 1944, for example, engineers were

The first flight of the Ariane 4 Rocket, launched from Kourou, French Guiana. *(Reproduced by permission of Photo Researchers, Inc.)*

exploring the possibility of using nuclear reactors to power rockets. A nuclear-powered rocket would carry a small nuclear reactor, the heat from which would be used to vaporize hydrogen gas. The hydrogen gas expelled from the rear of the rocket would provide its propulsive force. Calculations indicate that a nuclear rocket of this type would have a lifting force more than twice that of a traditional chemical rocket.

Other types of so-called low-thrust rockets have also been suggested. In some cases, the proposed propulsive force comes from atoms and molecules that have been ionized within the rocket body and then accelerated by being placed within a magnetic or electrical field. In other cases, a gas such as hydrogen is first turned into a plasma and then ionized and accelerated. As attractive as some of these ideas sound in theory, they have thus far found relatively few practical applications in the construction of rocket engines.

Missiles

The modern age of missile science can probably be said to have begun towards the end of World War II (1939–45). During this period, German rocket scientists developed the ability to produce vehicles that could deliver warheads to targets hundreds or thousands of miles from their launch point. For a period of time, it appeared that the German V-2 rocket-missile might very well turn the tide of the war and bring victory to Germany.

The cold war that followed the end of World War II provided a powerful incentive for the United States, the former Soviet Union, and a few other nations to spend huge amounts of money on the development of newer and more sophisticated missile systems. Missiles have the great advantage of being able to deliver a large destructive force at a great distance from the launch site. The enemy can be damaged or destroyed with essentially no damage to the party launching the missile.

As the cold war developed, however, it became obvious that the missile-development campaign was a never-ending battle. Each new development by one side was soon made obsolete by improvements in anti-missile defense mechanisms made by the other side. As a result, there is now a staggering variety of missile types with many different functions and capabilities.

Missile classification

Missiles can be classified in a number of different ways. Some are said to be unguided because, once they are launched, there is no further control over their flight. The German V-2 rockets were unguided missiles. Such missiles can be directed in the general vicinity of a target at the launch site, but once they are set off there is no further way that their path can be adjusted or corrected.

The vast majority of missiles, however, are guided missiles. This term refers to the fact that the missile's path can be monitored and changed either by instruments within the missile itself or by a guidance station.

Missiles can also be classified as aerodynamic or ballistic missiles. An aerodynamic missile is one equipped with wings, fins, or other structures that allow it to maneuver as it travels to its target. Aerodynamic missiles are also known as cruise missiles. Ballistic missiles are missiles that follow a free-fall path once they have reached a given altitude. In essence, a ballistic missile is fired into the air the way a baseball player makes a throw from the outfield, and the missile (the ball) travels along a path determined by its own velocity and Earth's gravitational attraction.

Finally, missiles can be classified according to the place from which they are launched and the location of their final target. V-2 rockets were surface-to-surface missiles since they were launched from a station on the ground in Germany and were designed to strike targets on the ground in Great Britain.

An air-to-air missile is one fired from the air (usually from an aircraft) with the objective of destroying another aircraft. One of the best known air-to-air missiles is the U.S. Sidewinder missile, first put into operation in 1956. The first Sidewinders were 2.84 meters (9.31 feet) long and 12.7 centimeters (5.00 inches) in diameter, with a weight of 75 kilograms (165 pounds) and a range of 1.1 kilometers (0.68 miles).

A surface-to-air missile is one fired from a ground station with the goal of destroying aircraft. The first surface-to-air missile used by the U.S. military was the Nike Ajax, a rocket with a weight of 1,042 kilograms (2,295 pounds), a length of 10.6 meters (34.8 feet), a diameter of 30.5 centimeters (12.0 inches), and a range of 48 kilometers (30 miles).

Some other types of missiles of importance to the military are antiship and anti-submarine missiles, both of which can be launched from ground stations, from aircraft, or from other ships. Military leaders were at one time also very enthusiastic about another type of missile, the antiballistic missile (ABM). The ABM program was conceived of as a large number of solid rockets that could be aimed at incoming missiles. U.S. engineers developed two forms of the ABM: the Spartan, designed for long-distance defensive uses, and the Spring, designed for short-range interception. The Soviet Union, in the meanwhile, placed its reliance on an ABM given the code name of Galosh. The ABM program came to a halt in the mid-1970s when the high cost of implementing a truly effective defensive system became apparent.

Structure of the missile

Any missile consists essentially of four parts: a body, known as the airframe (described above); the propulsive system; the weapon; and the guidance system. The propulsive systems used in missiles are the same as those described for rockets. That is, they consist of one or more liquid rockets, one or more solid rockets, or some combination of these.

In theory, missiles can carry almost any kind of high-explosive, chemical, biological, or nuclear weapon. Anti-tank missiles, as an example, carry very high-powered explosives that allow them to penetrate a 60-centimeter (24-inch) thick piece of metal. Nuclear weapons have, however, become especially popular for use in missiles. One reason, of course, is the destructiveness of such weapons. But another reason is that anti-missile jamming programs are often good enough to make it difficult for even the most sophisticated guided missile to reach its target without interference. Nuclear weapons cause destruction over such a wide area, however, that so-called defensive jamming is less important than it is with more conventional explosive warheads.

At one time, the methods used to guide a missile to its target were relatively simple. One of the most primitive of these systems was the use of a conducting wire trailed behind the missile and attached to a ground monitoring station. The person controlling the missile's flight could make adjustments in its path simply by sending electrical signals along the trailing wire. This system could be used, of course, only at a distance equal to the length of wire that could be carried by the missile, a distance of about 300 meters (1,000 feet).

The next step up from the trailing wire guidance system is one in which a signal is sent by radio from the guidance center to the missile. Although this system is effective at much longer ranges than the trailing wire system, it is also much more susceptible to interference (jamming) by enemy observers. Much of the essence of the missile battles that took place on paper during the cold war concerned finding new and more secure ways to send messages to a missile—and new and more sophisticated ways to interrupt and jam those signals.

Some missile systems carry their own guidance systems within their bodies. One approach is for the missile to send out radio waves aimed at its target and then to monitor and analyze the waves that are reflected back to it from the target. With this system, the missile can constantly make adjustments that keep it on its path to the target. As with ground-directed controls, however, a system such as this one is also subject to jamming by enemy signals.

Another guidance system makes use of a TV camera mounted in the nose of the missile. The camera is pre-programmed to lock in on the missile's target. Electronic and computer systems on board the missile can then keep the rocket on its correct path.

Rocks

Rocks are composed of minerals, which are natural inorganic (nonliving) substances with specific chemical compositions and structures. A rock may consist of many crystals of one mineral or combinations of many minerals. Hundreds of different kinds of minerals make up hundreds of different kinds of rocks. Geologists, scientists who study Earth and rocks, divide rocks into three main groups: igneous rocks, sedimentary rocks, and metamorphic rocks. These distinctions are made on the basis of the types of minerals in the rock, the shapes of individual mineral grains, and the overall texture of the rock. All of these properties indicate the environment, pressure, and temperature in which the rock formed.

Granite (left), an intrusive igneous rock, and obsidian (right), an extrusive igneous rock. Both samples are taken from the Sierra Nevada Mountains of California. *(Reproduced by permission of Photo Researchers, Inc.)*

Words to Know

Igneous rock: Rock formed from the cooling and hardening of magma.

Lava: Molten rock that occurs at the surface of Earth, usually through volcanic eruptions.

Magma: Molten rock found below the surface of Earth.

Metamorphic rock: Rock formed by transformation of preexisting rock through changes in temperature and pressure.

Mineral: A naturally occurring, inorganic substance with a definite chemical composition and structure.

Rock cycle: Processes through which rocks change from one type to another, typically through melting, metamorphism, uplift, weathering, burial, or other processes.

Sedimentary rock: Rock formed from compressed and solidified layers of organic or inorganic matter.

Weathering: Natural process that breaks down rocks and minerals at Earth's surface into simpler materials (sediment) by physical (mechanical) or chemical means.

Igneous rock

The first rocks on Earth were igneous rocks. Igneous rocks are formed by the cooling and hardening of molten material called magma. The word igneous comes from the Latin word *ignis,* meaning "fire." There are two types of igneous rocks: intrusive and extrusive. Intrusive igneous rocks form within Earth's crust: the molten material rises, filling any available crevices in the crust, and eventually hardens. These rocks are not visible until Earth above them has eroded away. A good example of intrusive igneous rock is granite. Extrusive igneous rocks form when the magma pours out onto Earth's surface or erupts at Earth's surface from a volcano. Once on the surface (where it is called lava), it begins to cool and the minerals in the rock crystallize or grow together so that the individual crystals lock together. Extrusive rocks are also called volcanic rocks. Basalt, formed from hardened lava, is the most common extrusive rock. Obsidian, a black, glassy rock, is also an extrusive rock.

Essentially, Earth's continents are slabs of granite sitting on top of molten rock. The crustal plates of Earth are continually shifting, being torn open by faults and altered by earthquakes and volcanoes. New igneous material is continually added to the crust, while old crust falls back into Earth, sometimes deep enough to be remelted. Igneous rocks are the source of many important minerals, metals, and building materials.

Sedimentary rock

Sedimentary rocks are those produced by the accumulation of sediments. These may be fine rock particles or fragments, skeletons of microscopic organisms, or minerals leached from rocks. Rock fragments and leached minerals are created through weathering, a natural process that breaks down rocks and minerals at Earth's surface into simpler materials by physical (mechanical) or chemical means.

Wind, water, ice, gravity, temperature changes, or a combination of these are all physical actions that break down preexisting rocks. Chemical weathering represents a second stage of rock disintegration in which small pieces of rock produced by physical weathering are then further

Stockbridge limestone is named after the town in Massachusetts where it is typically exposed. *(Reproduced by permission of Photo Researchers, Inc.)*

broken apart by chemical processes. Acid reactions are a common form of chemical weathering, and the most common such reactions occur when carbon dioxide and sulfur dioxide in the air react with water to form weak carbonic and sulfuric acid. Both of these acids have the ability to attack many kinds of rocks, changing them into other forms. For example, when carbonic acid reacts with limestone, it produces calcium bicarbonate.

The sediments created by weathering and the decay of organisms are then transported and deposited by wind, water, or ice. Over long periods of time, layer upon layer of sediments are deposited on top of each other and their own weight causes them to compress and harden into sedimentary rock. The horizontal layers of sedimentary rock are called strata. Common sedimentary rocks include shale, sandstone, and limestone.

Sedimentary rocks are the only rocks in which fossils can be preserved. The elevated temperatures and pressures needed to form both igneous and metamorphic rocks destroy fossils and organic remnants. The presence of fossils and the types of fossil organisms in a rock provide clues about the environment and age of sedimentary rocks. For example, fish fossils in sedimentary rock indicate that the sediments that make up the rock were deposited in a lake, river, or marine environment. By establishing the environment of the fossils in a rock, scientists learn more about the conditions under which the rock formed.

A sample of gneiss, a type of metamorphic rock, taken from the Sierra Nevada Mountains. *(Reproduced by permission of JLM Visuals.)*

Metamorphic rock

Metamorphic rock is rock that has changed from one type of rock into another. The word metamorphic comes from Greek and means "of changing form." Metamorphic rock is produced from igneous, sedimentary, or even other metamorphic rocks. Most of Earth's crust is made up of metamorphic rock. Igneous and sedimentary rocks become metamorphic rock as a result of intense heat from magma and pressure from burial within Earth. Although the rock undergoes extreme heat and a great deal of pressure, it does not melt. If the rock melted, it would become igneous and not metamorphic rock. Instead, the heat and pressure combine to change the mineral makeup of the rock. Essentially, metamorphic rocks are made of the same minerals as the original rock, but the various minerals have been rearranged to make a new rock.

There are two basic types of metamorphic rock: regional and thermal. Regional metamorphic rock, found mainly in mountainous regions, is formed by pressure. Different amounts of pressure produce different types of rock. The greater the pressure, the more drastic the change (also, the deeper the rock the higher the temperature, which adds to the potential for diverse changes). For example, a pile of mud can turn into shale (a fine-grained sedimentary rock) with relatively low pressure, about 3 miles (5 kilometers) down into Earth. With more pressure and some heat, shale can transform into slate and mica. Carried even deeper, slate transforms into schist (pronounced shist) and then gneiss (pronounced nice).

Thermal metamorphic rock, also called contact metamorphic rock, is formed by considerable pressure and, more important, intense heat. When molten rock pushes up into Earth's crust, the incredible pressure behind it forces the molten rock into any empty space. The accompanying intense heat causes the surrounding rock to completely recrystallize, forming a new rock. An example of this type of thermal metamorphic rock is marble, which is actually limestone whose calcite has recrystallized. Sandstone made mostly of quartz fragments recrystallizes into quartzite. Thermal metamorphic rocks are not as common or plentiful as regional metamorphic rocks.

The rock cycle

The rock cycle depicts how the three main rock types can change from one type to another. All rocks exposed at Earth's surface undergo weathering, forming sediments that can be deposited to form sedimentary rocks. As sedimentary rocks are buried beneath more sediment, they are subjected to increases in both pressure and temperature, which can result in metamorphism and the formation of metamorphic rock. If the temperature of metamorphism is extremely high, the rock might melt completely and later recrystallize as an igneous rock. Rocks can move through the rock cycle along other paths, but uplift or burial, weathering, and changes in temperature and pressure are the primary causes of changes in rocks from one type to another.

[*See also* **Coal; Minerals**]

Satellite

In astronomy, the word satellite refers to any single object that is orbiting another larger, more massive object under the influence of their mutual gravitational force.

A natural satellite is any celestial body orbiting a planet or star of larger size. The Moon is the natural satellite of Earth. The other solar

Intelsat VI floating over the Earth. *(Reproduced by permission of National Aeronautics and Space Administration.)*

system planets that have natural satellites (moons) are Mars (2), Jupiter (28), Saturn (18 known, additional 12 reported), Uranus (21), Neptune (8), and Pluto (1).

Artificial satellites are human-made devices that orbit Earth and other celestial bodies. These devices follow the same gravitational laws that govern the orbits of natural satellites. After being launched from Earth, artificial satellites are placed high enough to escape the denser parts of the atmosphere, which would slow down the orbit of the satellite and cause it to plummet to the ground. At the proper height, usually above 200 miles (320 kilometers), artificial satellites stay in orbit around Earth indefinitely. Those placed at this altitude take 90 minutes to circle Earth. The higher the altitude, the slower the satellite's orbit. At a height of 22,300 miles (36,000 kilometers), a satellite takes exactly 24 hours to circle Earth.

Artificial satellites orbiting Earth have been used to measure everything from the planet's weather to missile launches to the movements of ships. Communications satellites revolve about Earth in orbits 25,000 miles (40,225 kilometers) above the surface.

Artificial satellites have also been placed in orbit about the Moon, Mars, and Venus to provide detailed maps of their surfaces and to measure properties of their surrounding atmosphere.

[*See also* **Gravity and gravitation; Orbit; Solar system; Space probe**]

Saturn

Saturn, the sixth planet from the Sun, is named for the Roman god of agriculture, who was based on the Greek god Cronus. The second largest planet in the solar system, it measures almost 75,000 miles (120,600 kilometers) in diameter at its equator. Despite its large size, Saturn is the least dense of all the planets. It is almost 30 percent less dense than water; placed in a large-enough body of water, Saturn would float.

Saturn completes one rotation on its axis very quickly, roughly 10.5 Earth hours. As a result of this spinning, the planet has been flattened at its poles. The measurement around its equator is 10 percent greater than the measurement around the planet from pole to pole. In contrast to the length of its day, Saturn has a very long year. Lying an average distance of 887 million miles (1.4 billion kilometers) from the Sun, Saturn takes 29.5 Earth years to complete one revolution.

Saturn consists primarily of gas. Its hazy yellow clouds are made of crystallized ammonia, swept into bands by fierce, easterly winds that have been clocked at up to a speed of 1,100 miles (1,770 kilometers) per hour at its equator. Winds near the poles, however, are much tamer. Covering Saturn's surface is a sea of liquid hydrogen and helium that gradually becomes a metallic form of hydrogen. This sea conducts strong electric currents that, in turn, generate the planet's powerful magnetic field. Saturn's core, which is several times the size of Earth, is made of rock and ice. The planet's atmosphere is composed of about 97 percent hydrogen, 3 percent helium, and trace amounts of methane and ammonia. Scientists estimate the surface temperature to be about $-270°F$ ($-168°C$).

About every 30 years, following Saturn's summer, a massive storm takes place on the planet. Known as the Great White Spot, it is visible for nearly a month, shining like a spotlight on the planet's face. The spot then begins to break up and stretch around the planet as a thick white strip. The storm is thought to be a result of the warming of the

Saturn, the second largest planet in the solar system, and its system of rings. *(Reproduced by permission of National Aeronautics and Space Administration.)*

atmosphere, which causes ammonia to bubble up, solidify, and then be whipped around by the planet's monstrous winds.

Saturn's rings

Saturn's most outstanding characteristic are its rings. The three other largest planets (Jupiter, Uranus, and Neptune) also have rings, but Saturn's are by far the most spectacular. For centuries, astronomers thought the rings were moons. In 1658, Dutch astronomer Christiaan Huygens first identified the structures around Saturn as a single ring. In later years, equipped with stronger and stronger telescopes, astronomers increased the number of rings they believed surrounded the planet.

In 1980 and 1981, the *Voyager 1* and *Voyager 2* space probes sent back the first detailed photos of Saturn and its spectacular rings. The probes revealed a system of over 1,000 ringlets encircling the planet at a distance of 50,000 miles (80,450 kilometers) from its surface.

Saturn's rings, as seen by *Voyager* in November 1980. *(Reproduced by permission of National Aeronautics and Space Administration.)*

The rings, which are estimated to be one mile (1.6 kilometers) thick, are divided into three main parts: the bright A and B rings and the dimmer C ring. The A and B rings are divided by a gap called the Cassini Division, named for it discoverer, seventeenth-century French astronomer Giovanni Domenico Cassini. The A ring itself contains a gap, called the Encke Division after German astronomer Johann Encke, who discovered it in 1837. The Encke Division contains no matter, but the Voyager missions found that the Cassini Division contains at least 100 tiny ringlets, each composed of countless particles. Voyager confirmed the existence of puzzling radial lines in the rings called "spokes," which were first reported by amateur astronomers. Their nature remains a mystery, but may have something to do with Saturn's magnetic field. Saturn's outermost ring, the F ring, is a complex structure made up of several smaller rings along which "knots" are visible. Scientists speculate that the knots may be clumps of ring material, or mini moons.

While scientists do not know the full composition of the rings, they do know that the rings contain dust and a large quantity of water. The water is frozen in various forms, such as snowflakes, snowballs, hailstones, and icebergs. The forms range in size from about 3 inches (7.6 centimeters) to 30 feet (9 meters) in diameter. Scientists are also not sure how the rings were formed. One theory states that they were once larger moons that were smashed to tiny pieces by comets or meteorites. Another theory holds that the rings are pre-moon matter, cosmic fragments that never quite formed a moon.

Saturn's moons

Saturn has 18 known moons that have received officially sanctioned names from the International Astronomical Union. In late 2000, astronomers detected up to twelve possible new moons orbiting the planet, some at a distance between 6.2 and 12.4 million miles (10 and 20 million kilometers). These have all been given provisional designations, but scientists believe only six out of the twelve may turn out to be real moons. All the known moons are composed of about 30 to 40 percent rock and 60 to 70 percent ice. All but two have nearly circular orbits and travel around Saturn in the same plane.

Christiaan Huygens discovered Saturn's first moon Titan, in 1655. It is the only moon in the solar system with a substantial atmosphere, which is composed mainly of nitrogen. *Voyager 1* revealed that Titan may have seas of liquid methane bordered by organic tarlike matter. Titan's thick blanket of orange clouds, however, prevent a direct view of the surface.

Cassini mission to Saturn

The *Cassini* orbiter, which was launched in October 1997, will deliver much more information about Saturn and its moons. With a budget of $3.4 billion, it is the last of the National Aeronautics and Space Administration's (NASA) big-budget, big-mission planetary probes. *Cassini,* which weighs nearly 13,000 pounds (5,900 kilograms), carries 18 scientific instruments that will take a variety of measurements of Saturn's atmosphere, its moons, and the dust, rock, and ice that comprise its rings. After traveling some 2.2 billion miles (1 billion kilometers), the orbiter is scheduled to arrive at Saturn in mid-2004. It carries with it a probe, called *Huygens,* that was built by the European Space Agency. The probe will drop onto the surface of Titan for a detailed look at the moon's surface. If it survives the impact of its landing, *Huygens* will transmit data from the surface back to *Cassini* for up to 30 minutes. After releasing the probe, *Cassini* will orbit Saturn at least 30 times over a four-year period, gathering information and sending back more than 300,000 color images taken with an onboard camera.

[*See also* **Solar system**]

Savant

Savant is a name used to describe a person who has extraordinary skills in a very specialized area, but who is nonetheless intellectually disabled. It properly describes a rare phenomenon or syndrome in which a person with a severe mental handicap displays genius-like ability in a narrow field or area.

Shocking contrasts

The award-winning movie *Rain Man* brought attention to a mental condition in which a person, who is barely able to care for himself and who has trouble doing even the simplest tasks, can also be a prodigy in one specialized area. What distinguishes these rare individuals is that though mentally handicapped overall, they possess the ability to do one thing brilliantly, a talent that would be considered spectacular and extraordinary even if it were found in a person of normal abilities. It is a true puzzle to see a person who may be unable to interact normally with other people or who might never change his or her clothes or take a shower unless told, display phenomenal calculating, artistic, or musical ability.

Words to Know

Autism: A disorder in development characterized by an inability to relate socially to other people and a severe withdrawal from external reality.

Genius: Extraordinary mental ability or creative power.

Intelligence: The ability to solve problems and cope successfully with one's surroundings.

Testosterone: A male sex hormone that stimulates sperm production and is responsible for male sex characteristics.

First named

The term "idiot savant" was first coined in 1887 by British physician John Langdon Haydon Down (1828–1896), after whom the genetic disorder Down syndrome was named. At that time, doctors actually used the word "idiot" to describe someone whose IQ was below a certain level. Down linked this term to the French word "savant," meaning "learned one," and put together a term that captured the essence of this bizarre and seemingly contradictory syndrome.

One of the earliest accounts of this phenomenon was given by American physician Benjamin Rush (1746–1813), who is considered to be the father of American psychiatry. In 1789, Rush described the phenomenal calculating capability of a severely retarded man named Thomas Fuller who, Rush said, "could comprehend scarcely anything, either theoretical or practical, more complex than counting." One example he gave of Fuller's unique ability was his answer to the question, How many seconds a person had lived who was seventy years, seventeen days, and twelve hours old? Fuller thought for only 90 seconds, then gave the correct answer of 22,210,500,800 seconds, even correcting for the seventeen leap years involved.

Modern name

Today, the term "autistic savant" has mostly replaced the harsh-sounding "idiot savant," although others sometimes prefer the more generic "savant syndrome." A person who is autistic (pronounced awe-TIS-tik) or suffers from the neurological condition called autism (pronounced AWE-tizm) is extremely withdrawn, self-preoccupied, and barely interacts with others. Autistic individuals usually seem very strange to most people, as they sometimes have coordination problems and often display unusual, inappropriate, or exaggerated mannerisms and reactions. Their language, if expressed, may be bizarre, and altogether they usually cannot get by on their own. Autism is chronic, meaning that it does not go away, and it is incapacitating, meaning that even as adults, autistic people usually need constant supervision and support. When a person who is severely disabled in so many ways is able to do one thing at an extraordinary or even a prodigious level, it is both shocking and amazing.

Characteristics

Some of the things that a person with this syndrome can do will truly amaze us. The most common form of autistic savant are the mathematical calculators, some of whom display incredible calendar memory or who can calculate square roots and prime numbers in their heads with no hesitation.

Dustin Hoffman portrayed an autistic savant in the film *Rain Man*. (Reproduced by permission of The Kobal Collection.)

Some musical individuals have both perfect pitch and an endless memory for music. This means they can hear a complicated piece and immediately play it back perfectly from memory. Others are gifted artists. Despite these differences, there are certain characteristics that most share. First, this is a very rare condition, since by no means are all or even some autistic people so gifted. One author suggests that there may be no more than twenty-five or thirty "prodigious savants" living at present. A few artistic or musical savants are somewhat famous since they perform or exhibit their work.

Further, their special skills are always in an extremely deep but narrow range of abilities. For example, some of these great mathematical calculators do not possess even simple arithmetic skills. Another savant who had never received any musical instruction whatsoever could play anything she heard on a piano, yet still had the mental age of someone less than three years old. Also, in almost every case, there were very rigid limits as to what these people could actually do with the talent they had. So although one might be able to recite all manner of detail or facts about something, he or she would not be able to apply that information in any other way than the narrow method they were used to. Obviously, most of these impressive feats are tied in some way to memory, and almost all of these individuals have a phenomenal memory for detail. Finally, such persons are most often male, with the male-to-female ratio being roughly six-to-one.

Lack of theory

Medical science still does not have a single theory that is able to explain all the types of idiot savants. We do know that this condition can be both congenital (pronounced kon-JEN-ih-tul) meaning it exists at birth, or it can be caused or acquired through a certain type of brain injury or disease. One theory says that it is caused when the right side of the brain has to compensate for an injury of some sort to the left side. The skills associated with the brain's right hemisphere have more to do with concrete learning and artistic expression than the left side, whose skills are more abstract, logical, and symbolic. It is the right-side skills that the autistic savant possesses in great measure, while simultaneously possessing few or none of the left-side skills. Some speculate that this left-brain damage and right-brain compensation may occur while the individual is still a developing fetus. Others say that the high percentage of males suggests that the male hormone called testosterone (pronounced tess-TAHS-tur-own) is somehow involved during fetal development. However, all attempts to explain this phenomenon are still educated guesses, and most would readily admit that so far, science is completely baffled in trying to understand this amazing phenomenon.

Schizophrenia

Schizophrenia (pronounced skiht-zo-FREH-nee-uh) is a severe mental condition that interferes with normal thought processes, causing delusions, hallucinations, and mental disorganization. As the most common of the extremely serious mental disorders known as psychosis (pronounced sy-KO-sis), it affects men and women equally, is found all over the world, and is usually a long-term illness with no definite cure.

Its victims

Schizophrenia is described by the National Institute of Mental Health (NIMH) as a "chronic, severe, and disabling brain disease." NIMH estimates that approximately 1 percent of the American population at some point suffers from schizophrenia, meaning that more than two million Americans are considered to be schizophrenic in any given year. Others estimate that as many as half the patients in U.S. mental hospitals are schizophrenics. Although it occurs in women as often as in men, it seems to appear earlier in men, usually in their late teens or early twenties. Very young people, however, can sometimes be affected.

To be schizophrenic is to suffer from a profound disruption of cognition, meaning that the schizophrenic individual has a major problem with knowing and thinking. Some describe this condition as a thought disorder, and once we understand the sometimes terrifying symptoms that schizophrenics experience in their minds, we can better see why their perception of reality is often a distorted one. The mental disturbances they experience also affect their emotions, their actions, and even their language. People with schizophrenia often do not see or experience things the way most people do, and their world is often one of delusions and hallucinations. It is not unusual for them to hear "voices" or see things that are not really there. A common delusion or false personal belief of schizophrenics is that someone or something is controlling their thoughts or plotting against them. Hallucinations are false sensory experiences; a person experiencing hallucinations thinks he or she is seeing, hearing, or even touching something that in reality is not there or does not exist.

Delusions and hallucinations

Once we understand what schizophrenics are experiencing mentally, we should not be surprised when their behavior becomes strange or even bizarre. Often they are fearful and withdrawn, but other times their actions and speech can be frightening or at least very confusing to others.

Words to Know

Delusions: Incorrect beliefs about reality that are clearly false.

Hallucinations: Images, sounds, or odors that are seen, heard, or smelled by a person, but do not exist in reality.

Neurosis: Any emotional or mental disorder that affects only part of the personality, such as anxiety or mild depression, as a result of stress.

Neurotransmitter: A chemical that transmits electrical impulses (information) between nerve cells or nerve and muscle cells.

Psychosis: A major psychiatric disorder characterized by the inability to tell what is real from what is not real.

Other recognizable symptoms of schizophrenia are socially inappropriate behavior, dulled emotional responses, isolation and withdrawal that suggest a loss of any social interests, an inability to concentrate or "think straight," and a loss of a sense of self as a unique and separate individual. Since schizophrenics experience hallucinations and delusions of all sorts, they are often very frightened, anxious, and confused people. At times they may act totally detached and remote, sitting rigid for hours. Other times they may be highly agitated, moving constantly. They are understandably difficult to be with and are just as difficult to treat.

Historical evidence

Although some argue that schizophrenia is a modern disease, most agree that there is sufficient historical evidence to suggest that it is as old as humans. Stories of "mad" people whose behavior was beyond the limits or control of others and whose behavior was bizzare and unexplainable are found throughout the ancient history of all cultures. Ancient Babylonian documents are said to contain such evidence, and nearly 2,500 years ago, Greek historian Herodotus (480–425 B.C.) described the mad king of Sparta. In the second century A.D., Roman writer Celsus described three types of insanity, one of which sounds very much like schizophrenia. Many believe that schizophrenia was clearly described during the Middle Ages (period in European history from about A.D. 500 to 1500), and by the sixteenth century there are published accounts of clearly schizophrenic cases called "mania" or "melancolia." Some writers claim that the first printed description of schizophrenia was given by British physician Thomas Willis (1621–1675) when he described a certain type of "dementia."

Most agree, however, that the first modern description of symptoms now recognized as schizophrenia was given by German psychiatrist Emil Kraepelin (1856–1926) in 1896. Kraepelin's main contribution was his classification of mental illnesses, and it was Kraepelin who pointed out the difference between what is recognized today as manic-depressive psychosis and schizophrenia, which he called "dementia praecox" (pronounced deh-MEHN-shia PREE-cocks).

It was another German psychiatrist, however, who actually first suggested the term schizophrenia for the disease. In 1908, Eugen Bleuler (1857–1939) used the word schizophrenia in a paper he had written that was based on a study of 647 patients. Bleuler, who was a colleague of Austrian psychoanalyst Sigmund Freud (1856–1939), came up with the name to describe what he said was some sort of split in the proper functioning of the brain. He used the word split because he said that a schiz-

Positron Emission Tomography (PET) brain scans comparing a normal brain (left) with the brain of a schizophrenic (right). *(Reproduced by permission of Photo Researchers, Inc.)*

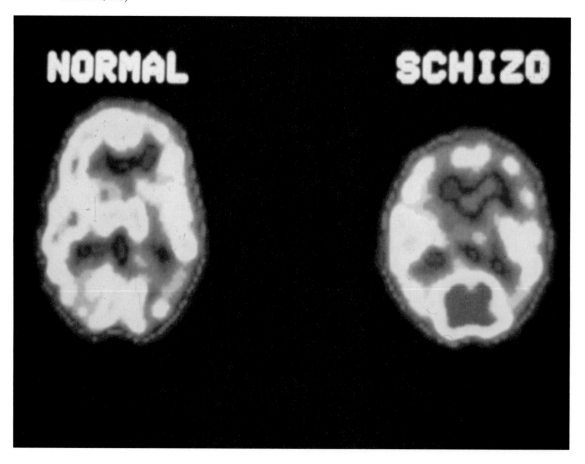

ophrenic's ideas are often isolated or separate from his feelings. Bleuler's new name for this condition was therefore derived from the Greek words for "split" and "mind" and soon replaced the older term dementia praecox. It should be noted, however, that schizophrenia is neither a condition exhibiting a "split personality" nor one of "multiple personalities." Rather, these rare conditions are considered to be a type of neurosis (pronounced nur-OH-sis) that is a less severe emotional disorder.

Types of schizophrenia

The main difference between schizophrenia and any other type of neurosis is that a neurosis is an emotional disorder, whereas schizophrenia is considered a form of organic brain disease, meaning that there is a physical (and not an emotional) reason why something is wrong. Until recently, science could only describe or categorize the different types of schizophrenia, and the categories offered by Kraepelin are still used. Paranoid schizophrenics typically suffer from delusions of persecution; the hebephrenic (pronounced hee-beh-FREN-ik) type has very disorganized thinking, difficulty in communicating, and shows inappropriate emotional responses (like laughing at a funeral); the catatonic schizophrenic suffers from uncontrollable bodily movements. In reality, many schizophrenics often display symptoms from each type.

Causes

Although there are a number of competing theories as to the causes of schizophrenia, no one explanation has yet been proven. Unfortunately, this means that there is no known single cause of schizophrenia. That does not mean, however, that science is completely baffled and helpless in trying to understand this brain disease. Some of the early, more psychoanalytical explanations suggested that people who lacked affection during infancy and early childhood became schizophrenic, but these psychological theories could not be proven.

Science then naturally moved to seek more physical explanations, and with twenty-first century advances in biomedical research and advanced imaging technologies, most theories now have a basis in biology. That is, they seek to find the primary cause or causes of schizophrenia in the body itself, specifically in the brain. For example, it has long been known that schizophrenia runs in families, and that individuals with a close relative who suffered from the disease have a greater chance of developing it than people who have no relatives with the illness. This suggests that there are some genetic factors involved, and that perhaps a genetic predisposition (a tendency toward something) makes some more susceptible than others. In fact, research on the human genome, which is the complete collection of genes found in a single set of human chromosomes, suggests that the defect may be found somewhere on chromosomes 13 and 6, although this has not yet been proven conclusively.

Despite this possible genetic link, scientists know for many reasons that genes cannot be the sole cause of schizophrenia. A good proof of this is a set of identical twins, only one of whom suffers from schizophrenia. More likely, schizophrenia does not have a single cause, but instead is determined by a combination of biological factors. Another major avenue of investigation is in the chemistry of the brain. This new research focuses on the brain's neurotransmitters (pronounced ner-o-trans-MIH-terz), which are substances that allow the neurons or nerve cells to communicate with one another. Investigators are therefore concentrating on the neurotransmitters called dopamine (pronounced DOPE-uh-meen) and glutamate (pronounced GLUE-tuh-mait) to find if too much or too little is important to schizophrenia.

Other scientists are using new brain-imaging techniques to examine the brains of living schizophrenics to try to find abnormalities in structure or function. They now know, for example, that schizophrenics have enlarged ventricles, which are fluid-filled cavities inside the brain. Another brain-related theory is that schizophrenia is caused by some sort of developmental disorder that happened when the fetus was still growing inside the mother's womb. Some suggest that this damage may stay hidden or dormant until puberty, when the brain's normal changes somehow activate them. Finally, another theory is that the disease is caused by a slow-acting virus.

Treatment

Since schizophrenia has no one known cause, the best medicine can do is to treat the symptoms. Before the 1950s, electroconvulsive treatment or shock therapy was the only known method of treatment. Since that time, various drugs have been used to try to minimize the symptoms of schizophrenia. Reserpine was the first drug to work, and it was based on a plant used in folk medicine to treat insomnia and insanity. Later, the new drug named Thorazine was developed. Both it and Reserpine were found to work by blocking the neurotransmitter dopamine. In the 1990s, a new group of antipsychotic drugs were produced that were very effective in keeping delusions and hallucinations under control, but they also left their patients emotionally empty and even reduced their normal motivation.

Opposite Page: A colored Positron Emission Tomography (PET) brain scans of a schizophrenic while speaking versus normal patient while speaking. *(Reproduced by permission of Photo Researchers, Inc.)*

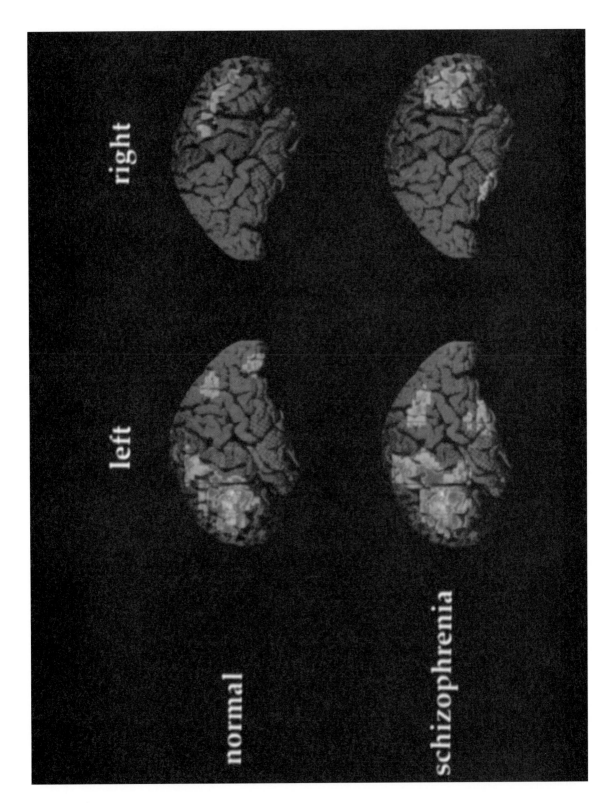

right

left

normal

schizophrenia

Today, doctors are able to give new antipsychotic drugs in more calibrated or finely-tuned dosages so that they work to minimize the terrors, but do not put the person in a complete "emotional straitjacket." With their "demons" under better control, schizophrenics are able to deal with the everyday world in a more rational way. The key to every schizophrenic's health is to keep strictly to his or her treatment plan. However, although these new drugs are far better than the old ones, they still pose a long-term risk that the patient may develop serious side-effects involving the muscles.

Despite all the treatment, research, and gains in understanding, the fact remains that today's treatment for schizophrenia has limits. Very often, no matter how symptom-free the patient is, he or she may still have problems being "normal" in ways that matter—like caring for themselves, communicating with others, being motivated, and most important of all, establishing and keeping relationships with other people. It has been shown, however, that for patients whose symptoms are under control, the help and understanding they receive from their family, friends, and even self-help and support groups goes a long way toward making them better able to manage their condition. Continued understanding is needed as much as continued research.

[*See also* **Psychiatry; Psychosis; Tranquilizer**]

Scientific method

The term scientific method refers in general to the procedures that scientists follow in obtaining true statements about the natural world. As it happens, scientists actually use all manner of procedures to obtain the information they want. Some of those procedures are not very objective, not very formal, and not very systematic. Still, the "ground rules" by which science tends to operate are distinctive and very different from those by which "true statements" are produced in philosophy, the arts, history, ethics, and other fields of human endeavor.

"The scientific method"

Many science textbooks begin with an exposition of a system of thought that, at least in the ideal, describes the way scientists work. The system is actually a cyclical process, one in which it is impossible to say where the whole process begins.

Certainly one element in the process is the recognition of a problem or the desire to know something specific about the natural world. For ex-

Words to Know

Experiment: A controlled observation.

Fact: A statement that is widely accepted as being true by scientists.

Hypothesis: An idea phrased in the form of a statement that can be tested by observation and/or experiment.

Scientific law: A statement that brings together and shows the relationship of many scientific facts.

Scientific theory: A statement that brings together and shows the relationship of many scientific laws; also, but less commonly, another term for hypothesis.

ample, one might wonder whether an airplane flies better with narrow wings or broad wings. In most cases, a scientist poses a question such as this in terms of a hypothesis. A hypothesis is an idea phrased in the form of a statement that can be tested by observation and/or experimentation. In this example, the hypothesis might be: "Airplanes with broad wings fly better than airplanes with narrow wings."

The next step in the procedure is to devise ways of testing that hypothesis. In some cases, one can simply go out into the real world and collect observations that will confirm or deny the hypothesis. In most cases, however, a scientist will design one or more experiments to test the hypothesis. An experiment is really nothing more than a set of procedures designed to test a given hypothesis. Experiments are generally more productive than observations in the natural world because they deal with only one specific aspect of the whole world. Confusing factors can be intentionally omitted in order to concentrate on the one factor in which the scientist is interested.

In the case of airplane wings, one approach would be to design a series of airplanes, each with wings somewhat broader than the others. Each plane could be flown, and the efficiency of its flight noted.

The results of observations and/or experiments permit scientists to draw conclusions about the hypothesis. In our example, a scientist might discover that airplanes with broad wings fly better or not as well as airplanes with narrow wings. Or the results of experimentation may indicate that flying efficiency seems unconnected to wing width.

Imagine that a scientist, however, discovers that every broad-winged airplane flies better than every narrow-winged plane tested. Can it then be said that the original hypothesis has been confirmed?

Probably not. One critical aspect of science is that no hypothesis is regarded as true until it has been tested and re-tested many times. If two dozen scientists all perform the same experiment and get the same result, then confidence in the truth of that result grows. After a long period of testing, a hypothesis may begin to take on the form of a fact. A fact is a statement that is widely accepted as being true by scientists.

Interestingly enough, it is never possible in science to prove a statement true for all time. The best one can hope for is that a fact is not proved wrong. That is, maybe the one-hundred-first time a fact/hypothesis is tested, it is found to be incorrect. That single instance does not necessarily prove the fact/hypothesis wrong, but it does raise questions. If additional "false" results are obtained, the hypothesis is likely to be rejected as "not true."

The cycle of the scientific method is completed when a new fact has been learned. In most cases, that new fact will suggest new questions, new hypotheses in the minds of scientists. For example, if broad-winged airplanes do fly more efficiently than narrow-wing airplanes, then what is the effect of making the wings fatter or thinner? As soon as that question (or one like it) occurs to someone, the cycle of hypothesizing, testing, and concluding begins all over again.

Laws and theories

Obviously, untold numbers of facts exist in science. The process of learning a new science is, to a large extent, learning the facts that make up that science.

But individual facts in and of themselves are not very useful in science. Their greater importance lies in the variety of ways in which they can be combined to make more general statements about nature. For example, it might be possible to make a factual statement about the boiling point of ethyl alcohol, a second factual statement about the boiling point of propyl alcohol, a third factual statement about the boiling point of butyl alcohol, and so on. But what is of greater interest to scientists is some general statement about the boiling points of *all* alcohols in general. General statements that bring together many, many related facts are known as scientific laws.

Scientific laws, like individual facts, often suggest new questions, new hypotheses, new experiments, and, eventually, new facts. These facts tend to make scientists more confident about the truth of a law or, in some cases, raise questions as to the law's correctness.

One more step of generalization exists in science: scientific theories. A great deal of confusion centers on the word "theory" in science. Most people use the word theory to suggest a guess about something: "I have a theory as to who stole that money." Scientists sometimes use the word in the same sense.

But theory can mean something quite different in science. A scientific theory is a system of generalization even larger and more comprehensive than a scientific law. Just as a law is a collection of facts, so a scientific theory is a collection of scientific laws.

This definition explains the misunderstanding that some nonscientists have about the use of the word theory. Some people may believe that the theory of evolution is only a guess, as the term is used in everyday life. But the word theory is not used in that sense here. The theory of evolution refers to a massive system that brings together many, many laws that describe the way organisms change over time. Biologists are not guessing that these laws are true; they are supremely confident that they are, in fact, true.

What science can and cannot do

The scientific method has been a powerful tool for learning a great deal about the physical world, but it is not a system for answering all questions. The only questions science can attack are those that can be answered by using the five human senses in one way or another. For example, suppose that someone hypothesizes that the reason earthquakes occur is that tiny invisible demons living under Earth's surface cause those events. That hypothesis is, by definition, untestable by scientific methods. If the demons are invisible, there is no way for scientists to observe them. One might look for indirect evidence of the demons' existence, but the problem is probably beyond scientific investigation.

It is for this reason that topics such as love, hope, courage, ambition, patriotism, and other emotions and feelings are probably beyond the scope of scientific research. That statement does not mean these topics are not worth studying—just that the scientific method is not likely to produce useful results.

Another question that the scientific method cannot solve is "why?" That statement may startle readers because most people think that explaining why things happen is at the core of scientific research.

But saying why something happens suggests that we know what is in the mind of someone or something that makes events occur as they do.

A long time ago, scientists decided that such questions could not be part of the scientific enterprise. We can describe how the Sun rises, how objects fall, how baseballs travel through the air, and so on. But science will never be able to explain why these things occur as they do.

Seasons

Seasons on Earth are characterized by differences in temperature and the length of daylight. The four distinct seasons—spring, summer, autumn (or fall), and winter—are found only in the temperate zones. These zones extend from 23.5 degrees North (and South) latitude to 66.5 degrees North (and South) latitude. The equatorial regions or torrid zones have no noticeable seasonal changes, only a wet season and a dry season. Polar regions experience only a light season and a dark season.

Spring comes from an Old English word meaning "to rise." Summer originated as a Sanskrit word meaning "half year" or "season." Autumn comes originally from a Etruscan word for "maturing." Winter comes from an Old English word meaning "wet" or "water."

In the Northern Hemisphere, astronomers assign an arbitrary starting date for each season. Spring begins around March 21, summer around June 22, autumn around September 23, and winter around December 22. In the Southern Hemisphere, the seasons are reversed with spring beginning in September, summer in December, fall in March, and winter in

The seasons. *(Reproduced by permission of The Gale Group.)*

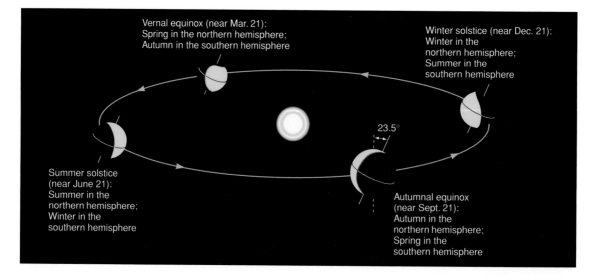

Vernal equinox (near Mar. 21):
Spring in the northern hemisphere;
Autumn in the southern hemisphere

Winter solstice (near Dec. 21):
Winter in the
northern hemisphere;
Summer in the
southern hemisphere

23.5°

Summer solstice
(near June 21):
Summer in the
northern hemisphere;
Winter in the
southern hemisphere

Autumnal equinox
(near Sept. 21):
Autumn in the
northern hemisphere;
Spring in the
southern hemisphere

↓ Words to Know

Autumnal equinox: Date in the fall of the year when Earth experiences 12 hours of daylight and 12 hours of darkness, usually around September 23.

Summer solstice: Date on which the Sun is highest in the sky at noon in the Northern Hemisphere, usually around June 22.

Temperate zones: Two regions on Earth bounded by 23.5 degrees latitude and the 66.5 degrees latitude.

Torrid zone: Zone on Earth bounded by 23.5 degrees north and south latitude.

Vernal equinox: Date in the spring of the year when Earth experiences 12 hours of daylight and 12 hours of darkness, usually around March 21.

Winter solstice: Date on which the Sun's noontime height is at its lowest in the Northern Hemisphere, usually on December 22.

June. Seasons in the Southern Hemisphere are generally milder because of the larger amounts of ocean surface in that hemisphere. Since oceans heat up and cool down much slower than landmasses, they exert a moderating force on temperatures.

Reason for the seasons

Earth makes one complete revolution about the Sun each year. Changes in the seasons are caused not by the varying distance between Earth and the Sun, but by the tilt of Earth on its axis during that revolution. (Earth's axis of rotation is tilted 23.5 degrees to the plane of its orbit.) As Earth orbits the Sun, there are times of the year when the North Pole is alternately tilted toward the Sun (during Northern Hemispheric summer) or tilted away from the Sun (during Northern Hemispheric winter). At other times the axis is generally parallel to the incoming Sun's rays.

During summer, two effects contribute to produce warmer weather. First, the Sun's rays fall more directly on Earth's surface, producing a stronger heating effect. Second, daylight hours outnumber nighttime hours. The Sun's rays warm Earth during daylight hours and Earth cools at night by reradiating heat back into space. Since there are longer periods of daylight and shorter periods of darkness during the summer, Earth receives more solar heat then it releases back into space. Thus, areas experiencing summer stay warmer.

The equinox

When the axis of Earth is perfectly parallel to the incoming rays of the Sun in spring—around March 21—the Sun rises in a direction that is due east everywhere on Earth and stands directly over the equator at noon. As a result, daylight hours equal nighttime hours everywhere on Earth. This effect gives rise to the name given to this date, the vernal equinox. Vernal comes from the Latin word for "spring," while equinox is formed from the Latin word for "equal night." The corresponding date in the fall when 12 hours of daylight and 12 hours of darkness occur everywhere on Earth—around September 23—is known as the autumnal equinox.

The solstice

After the vernal equinox, the Sun continues to move in a northward direction and rise a little farther north of east each day until around June 22. On this day, the Sun has reached its extreme northward position and seems to stand still in its noon height above the horizon. For this reason, the date is known as the summer solstice, from the Latin words meaning "sun stands still." The summer solstice, the longest day and shortest night of the year in the Northern Hemisphere, marks the beginning of summer in the Northern Hemisphere. Afterward, the Sun begins to move southward. It crosses the celestial equator (the autumnal equinox) and continues to move southward, rising a little farther south of east each day until it reaches its most extreme southward position around December 22—the winter solstice (the shortest day and longest night in the Northern Hemisphere). Afterward, the Sun begins its northward movement back to the vernal equinox.

Celebrating the seasons

Early societies celebrated the changes in the seasons on some of these cardinal dates. The vernal equinox was a day of celebration for the early Celtic tribes in ancient England, France, and Ireland. Other northern European tribes also marked the return of warmer weather on this date. Even the winter solstice was a time to celebrate, as it marked the lengthening days that would lead to spring. The ancient Romans celebrated the Feast of Saturnalia on the winter solstice. And even though there are no historical records to support the choice of a late December date for the birth of Jesus of Nazareth, Christians in the fourth century A.D. chose to celebrate Jesus' birth on the winter solstice. In the Julian calendar system in use at that time, this date fell on December 25.

[*See also* **Calendar; Global climate**]

Seed

A seed is a part of a flowering plant involved in reproduction. It consists of three major parts: the embryo, endosperm, and testa. The embryo is produced when male and female elements are combined during reproduction. It will eventually grow into a new plant. The endosperm is a collection of stored food the young plant will use as it begins to germinate, or grow. The testa is a tough outer layer that protects the embryo and endosperm from damage by outside factors.

Two kinds of seed plants exist. Gymnosperms are plants that produce naked seeds. The most common type of gymnosperms are conifers, cone-bearing trees and shrubs such as firs, hemlocks, junipers, larches, pines, and spruce. Angiosperms are plants whose seeds are enclosed in a protective structure called the fruit. Angiosperms are also known as flowering plants because they produce flowers in which seeds are produced and in which they develop.

Seed production

Seeds are produced when pollen is released from the male (stamen) part of a plant. That pollen comes into contact with the ovules of the female (pistil) parts of a plant. Some kinds of plants contain both male and female organs on the same plant. In that case, self-fertilization can occur when pollen from one part of the plant fertilizes ovules on another part of the same plant.

In most plants, fertilization occurs between two different plants, one of which contains only male flowers and the other only female flowers. This process requires some kind of mechanism by which pollen can be carried between plants. In some cases, movement of air (wind) can bring about this kind of fertilization. Insects and birds can also produce the same result. For example, a bee may visit a male plant in search of nectar. In that search, the bee may rub off pollen onto its body. When the bee then visits a female plant, it may release that pollen onto the ovules of the second plant, making fertilization possible.

Words to Know

Angiosperm: A plant whose seeds are enclosed in a protective structure called the fruit.

Dispersal: Any process by which seeds are spread outward from their parent plant.

Dormancy: A state of inactivity in an organism.

Embryo: The young form of an organism.

Endosperm: A collection of stored food used by a young plant during germination.

Germination: The beginning of growth of a seed.

Gymnosperm: A plant that produces naked seeds.

Pistil: The female reproductive organ in a plant.

Pollination: The transfer of pollen from the male organ of a plant to the female organ.

Self-fertilization: The process in which pollen from one part of a plant fertilizes ovules on another part of the same plant.

Stamen: The male reproductive organ in a plant.

Testa: A tough outer layer that protects the embryo and endosperm of a seed from damage.

The endosperm within a seed is used when the embryo begins to develop. Seeds vary widely in terms of the relative amounts of embryo and endosperm they may contain. For example, members of the orchid family have tiny, dustlike seeds that consist of little more than core embryonic tissues, with very little in the way of energy reserves. In contrast, the gigantic seeds of some coconuts can weigh more than 60 pounds (25 kilograms), most of which is nutritional reserve surrounded by fibrous, protective husk.

Seed dispersal

A seed exists in a dormant (sleeping) state. It begins to germinate, or grow, only when it is deposited in a favorable environment, such as moist, warm ground. The long process by which a seed changes from a tiny embryo into a fully grown plant requires time and favorable conditions. In most cases, young plants have a better chance to survive and grow if they are deposited at some distance from the parent plant. In those cases, they will not have to compete for sunlight, water, and nutrients with their own parents.

There are, however, some important exceptions to this general rule. For example, the adults of annual species of plants die at the end of their breeding season. In those cases the parent plants do not compete with their seeds. Nevertheless, even annual plants tend to disperse their seeds widely.

Methods of dispersal. Plants have evolved a variety of mechanisms to disperse their seeds effectively. In some plant species, seeds are very buoyant, so they can be dispersed over great distances by the winds. Some well-known examples of this kind of plant are the fluffy seeds of the dandelion and fireweed. The seeds of maple trees are also dispersed by the wind. These seeds have a one-sided wing that causes them to swirl propeller-like after they are released from a parent tree. This structure allows maple seeds to be carried by even light breezes some distance from their parent before they hit the ground.

Some plants have developed an interesting method of dispersal, known as tumbleweeding. These plants grow into a roughly spherical shape. After the seeds are ripe, the mature plant detaches from the ground surface and is then blown about by the wind, shedding its seeds widely as it tumbles along.

The seeds of many other species of plants are dispersed by animals. Some seeds have structures that allow them to attach to the fur or feathers of passing animals, who then carry the seeds some distance away from the parent plant before they are deposited to the ground. One example of this mechanism is burdock, whose spherical fruits have numerous hairs with tiny hooked tips that stick to fur. This fruit also sticks to human clothing, and was the botanical model that inspired the invention of Velcro™, a sticky, synthetic fastening material.

Another mechanism by which seeds are dispersed by animals involves their encasement in a fleshy, edible fruit. Such fruits are often brightly colored, have pleasant odors, and are nutritious and attractive to herbivorous (plant-eating) animals. These animals eat the fruit, seeds and all. After the fruit passes through the animal's digestive system, the seeds are dispersed at some distance from the parent plant.

The seeds of many plants with this sort of animal-dispersal strategy actually require passage through the gut of an animal before they will germinate. Some familiar examples of species that develop animal-dispersed fruits include the cherries, tomatoes, and watermelon.

Seed germination

After seeds have been dispersed into the environment, they may remain in a dormant state for some time, until appropriate cues are sensed for germination. Such clues include sufficient water, oxygen, and an appropriate temperature. Interestingly enough, the seeds of many species will not germinate even under favorable conditions. For example, seeds produced and dispersed just before the beginning of a cold season might actually experience the right conditions for germination for a short period of time. However, they would probably not survive if they germinated at once. A period of dormancy enables the seeds to wait out the cold season, and to begin growth when conditions are more favorable for the mature plant, in the springtime. It allows seeds a better chance of surviving unfavorable conditions and developing successfully into plants.

Germination begins with an increase of metabolic activity within the seed (that is, organic compounds are broken down to produce energy). The first visible sign of germination in angiosperms is generally an enlargement of the seed. That enlargement is caused by an intake of water from the environment. The seed's covering may wrinkle and crack at this

A close-up of grass seed growing on the tip of a blade of grass. *(Reproduced by permission of The Stock Market.)*

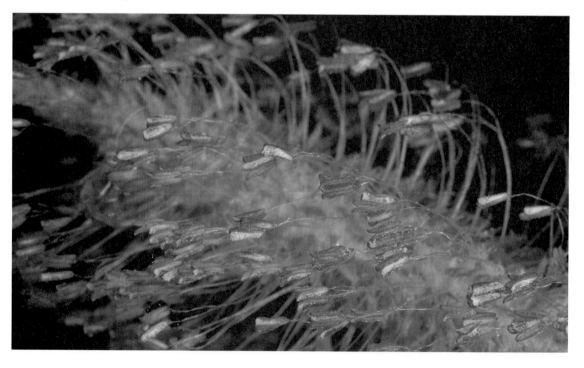

time. Soon afterward, the embryonic root emerges from the seed and begins to grow down into the soil. At about this time the shoot also emerges and grows upward out of the soil.

Uses of seeds

Seeds are used by humans for a number of purposes. The most important of those uses are as foods. Some seeds are eaten directly, while other are used to manufacture flour, starch, oil, alcohol, or some other edible products. Some examples of such seeds include those of wheat, rice, maize, sorghum, barley, peanut, soybean, lentil, common pea, common bean, coconut, walnut, pecan, and sunflower.

Many other seeds are eaten with their fruits, although it is generally the encasing fruit walls that are the sought-after source of nutrition. A few examples of edible fruits include those of the pumpkin or squash, bell pepper, apple, sweet cherry, strawberry, raspberry, and sweet orange.

[*See also* **Plant; Reproduction**]

Set theory

A set is a collection of things. A set can consist of real or literal numbers (such as 1, 2, 3, 4 or a, b, c, d) or of objects (such as baseballs or books). Set theory is the field of mathematics that deals with the properties of sets that are independent of the things that make up the set. For example, a mathematician might be interested in knowing about sets S and T without caring at all whether the two sets are made of baseballs, books, letters, or numbers.

The things that do to make up a set are called members or elements. In the above examples, 1, 2, 3, and 4 are members or elements of one set, and a, b, c, and d are elements of a second set.

Sets can be made of anything at all. The only characteristic they must have in common is classification together in a set. For example, the collection of all the junk at a rummage sale is a perfectly good set. These items may have little in common, except that someone has gathered them up and put them in a rummage sale. That act is enough to make the items a set.

Properties of sets

Set theory is based on a few basic definitions and fairly obvious properties of sets. The statements below summarize the most fundamental of these definitions and properties.

Words to Know

Complement: That part of a set S that is not contained in a particular subset T.

Difference: That part of a set S that is not in a set T.

Element: Any member of a set.

Intersection: A set comprised of all the elements common to two or more sets.

Set: A collection of objects, physical or abstract.

Subset: A set T in which every member of T is also a member of some other set S.

Union: The set that contains all the elements found in either of both of two sets.

Definition of a set. A set is usually defined by naming it with an upper case Roman letter (such as S) followed by the elements of the set. For example, the items in a rummage sale might be indicated as S = {basketball, horseshoe, scooter, bow tie, hockey puck}, in which the braces ({}) enclose the members of the set.

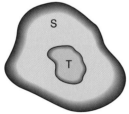

Figure 1.   T is a subset of S

Equality of sets. Two sets are said to be equal if every element in each set is also an element of the second set. In other words, two sets are equal if, and only if, they both contain the same elements.

Subsets. One set (call it T) is said to be a subset of a second set (call it S) if every element in T is also contained in S AND if some elements in S are not included in T. This condition is illustrated in Figure 1. The portion of S that is not included in T is known as the complement of T. It consists of all of the elements contained in S but not contained in T. Figure 2 illustrates the idea of a complement of a set.

Figure 2.   The complement of T

Union of sets. The union of two sets is defined as the collection of elements that belong to (1) either of the two sets or (2) both of the two sets. In other words, the union of the two sets corresponds to the sum of all their elements. Figure 3 shows the union of two sets, S and T.

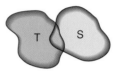

The union of T and S   Figure 3.

Intersection of sets. The intersection of two sets is defined as the collection of elements that belong to both of the two sets. In Figure 4, for example, the more heavily shaded area shows the elements that are contained in both S and T. The lighter shaded areas represent elements that belong to S, but not to T, or to T, but not to S.

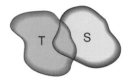

The intersection of T and S   Figure 4.

Difference of two sets. The difference between two sets is defined as the collection of elements that belong in one set but not in the other. The more darkly shaded portion of Figure 5 shows the difference S-T. Notice that it contains all of the elements of S with the exception of the small portion that also belongs to T.

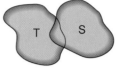

The difference S - T

Figure 5. *(Reproduced by permission of The Gale Group.)*

Sexually transmitted diseases

Long known as venereal disease, after Venus, the Roman goddess of love, sexually transmitted diseases (STDs) are among the most common infectious diseases in the world. (An infectious disease is one caused by a parasite that attacks a host and begins to multiply, interfering with the normal life functions of the host.) There are more than 20 known STDs, ranging from life-threatening to painful and unsightly.

While acquired immunodeficiency syndrome (AIDS) is the most widely publicized STD, others are more common. Chlamydia, gonorrhea, and genital warts are nearing epidemic rates in the United States. Other common STDs include genital herpes, trichomoniasis, and chancroid (pronounced KAN-kroyd). STDs are most prevalent among teenagers and young adults under the age of 25 and affect individuals of all backgrounds and socioeconomic levels. Some STDs are caused by bacteria and usually can be

Words to Know

Antibiotic: Drugs used to fight infections.

Bacteria: Single-celled microorganisms that live in soil, water, plants, and animals, and some of which are agents of disease.

Cervix: In females, the opening where the vagina meets the uterus.

Chancre: A sore that occurs in the first stage of syphilis at the place where the infection entered the body.

Epidemic: A rapidly spreading outbreak of a contagious disease.

Genitals: Organs of the reproductive system.

Infectious disease: A condition that results when a parasitic organism attacks a host and begins to multiply, interfering with the normal life functions of the host.

Urethra: The canal that carries urine from the bladder and serves as a genital duct.

Uterus: A pear-shaped, hollow muscular organ in which a fetus develops during pregnancy.

Vagina: In females, the muscular tube extending from the uterus to the outside of the body.

Virus: An infectious agent that can only reproduce in the cells of a living host.

Vulva: The external parts of the female genital organs.

treated and cured. Others are caused by viruses and can typically be treated but not cured. Untreated STDs pose an enormous public health problem.

Bacterial STDs

STDs caused by bacteria include syphilis, gonorrhea, chlamydia, and chancroid. Syphilis is usually spread through sexual contact and begins with painless lesions (sores) called chancres (pronounced KAN-kerz) that may appear inside or outside the body. The disease occurs in four stages and eventually affects the entire body. It is curable with the antibiotic penicillin but if left untreated can result in blindness, insanity, or death.

Gonorrhea is a common infectious disease that often has no initial symptoms. It affects the urinary tract and reproductive organs in males and females and, if left untreated, can cause sterility and blindness. Chlamydia infection is the most common sexually transmitted disease in the United States. Symptoms of chlamydia are similar to those of gonorrhea, and the disease can result in sterility in both males and females if left untreated. Chancroid is a bacterial disease that is more common in males and is characterized by painful ulcers and inflamed lymph nodes in the groin. Syphilis, gonorrhea, chlamydia, and chancroid can all be successfully treated with antibiotics.

Viral STDs

Viral STDs include AIDS, genital herpes, and genital warts. AIDS is caused by the human immunodeficiency virus (HIV), which attacks the immune system, making the body susceptible to infections and rare

The progression of a sexually transmitted disease (STD). *(Reproduced by permission of The Gale Group.)*

SEXUAL ACTIVITY

The odds of developing sexually transmitted disease (STD) can be reduced significantly depending on choices made concerning when and how to have sexual activity. The safest option is to avoid sexual activity with individuals who are at high risk of an STD, or with those who have a sexually transmitted disease. Individuals can also choose a condom during sexual activity, which provides some protection against many STDs. They may also choose to limit the number of people with whom they have sex or to avoid sex entirely.

EXPOSURE

Once one has been exposed to an STD, various factors affect whether one develops the disease. Individuals with other STDs appear to be more vulnerable to developing STDs. The type of body part exposed to the disease also plays a role in whether one will develop an STD. In general, exposure to open cuts or sores makes one more likely to develop an STD. Also, genetic predisposition to STDs plays a role in who develops the disease.

TRANSMISSION

FURTHER TRANSMISSION AND COMPLICATIONS

BACTERIAL INFECTION

The nature of STDs determines how difficult they will be to treat successfully. Bacterial STDs, such as syphilis and gonorrhea, can generally be treated successfully when found promptly.

VIRAL INFECTION

The STDs that are caused by viruses can not be cured, though some can be relieved through medication. These include AIDS and herpes. The inability of modern medicine to cure these viral infections means they can be transmitted even after individuals receive medical treatment. While many STDs can be cured, others become a part of life.

cancers. HIV is transmitted through the exchange of bodily fluids, such as semen, vaginal fluids, or blood. AIDS is a fatal disease in which a person usually dies from an infection that the body's damaged immune system cannot fight off.

Genital herpes is a widespread, recurrent viral infection caused by one of two types of herpes simplex virus. Herpes simplex virus type 1 most frequently causes cold sores of the lips or mouth. Herpes simplex virus type 2 causes painful blisters in the genital area (reproductive organs). After an initial painful infection that lasts about three weeks, recurring outbreaks of about ten days' duration may occur a few times a year.

Genital warts are caused by the human papillomavirus, of which there are more than 60 strains. After becoming infected with the virus through sexual contact, genital warts usually develop within two months. They may appear on the vulva, cervix, or vaginal wall of females and in the urethra or foreskin of the penis in males. The warts can be removed in various ways, but the virus remains in the body. Genital warts are associated with cancer of the cervix in females.

STDs caused by viruses cannot be cured. Currently, experimental AIDS and herpes vaccines are being tested with the hope that they will provide immunity against these diseases.

Infection on the back of a man with late-stage syphilis. (Reproduced by permission of Phototake.)

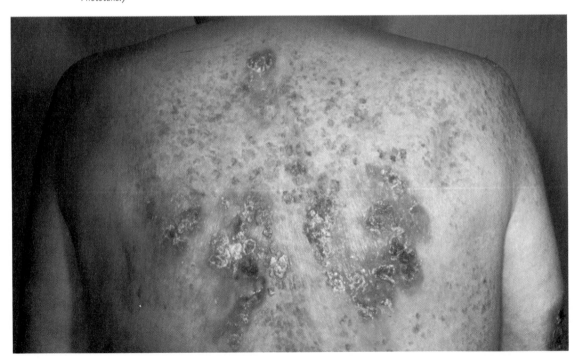

Other STDs

Other STDs include trichomoniasis, an infection caused by a parasitic protozoan that produces inflammation of the vagina and a bad-smelling, foamy discharge in females. It can also infect the urinary tract of both males and females. Treatment consists of administration of a drug that kills the protozoa.

Prevention

The only sure way to prevent contracting an STD is through sexual abstinence. Other methods that can aid in prevention and spread of STDs include the use of condoms, knowledge of the physical signs and symptoms of disease, and having regular check-ups.

[*See also* **AIDS (acquired immunodeficiency syndrome); Bacteria; Virus**]

Skeletal system

Inside every person is a skeleton, a sturdy framework of 206 bones. The skeleton protects the body's organs, supports the body, and provides attachment points for muscles to enable body movement. Bones also produce blood cells and act as a storage site for minerals such as calcium and phosphorus.

All humans are born with over 300 bones. But some bones, such as those in the skull and lower spine, fuse (join together) during growth, thereby reducing the number. The skeletal system is made up of living material, with networks of blood vessels running throughout. Living mature bone is about 60 percent calcium compounds and about 40 percent collagen (a fibrous protein). Hence, bone is strong, hard, and slightly elastic. Although mature bones consist largely of calcium, most bones in the human skeleton began as cartilage. Cartilage is a type of connective tissue that contains collagen and elastin fibers.

Individual bones meet at areas called joints and are held in place by connective tissue. Cartilage lines the surface of many joints and helps reduce friction between bones. The connective tissues linking the skeleton together at the joints are ligaments and tendons. Both are made up of collagen, but serve different functions. Ligaments link bones together and help prevent dislocated joints. Tendons link bone to muscle.

Because the bones making up the human skeleton are inside the body, the skeleton is called an endoskeleton. Some animals, such as the crab, have an external skeleton called an exoskeleton.

Structure

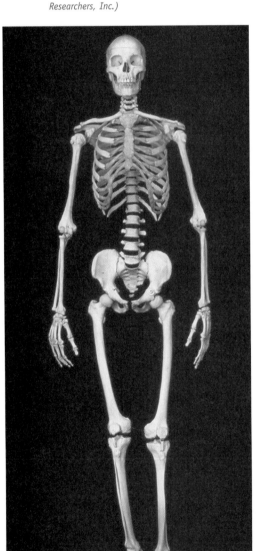

A frontal view of the human skeleton. *(Reproduced by permission of Photo Researchers, Inc.)*

The human skeletal system is divided into two main groups: the axial skeleton and the appendicular skeleton. The axial skeleton includes bones associated with the body's main axis, the spine. This includes the spine, the skull, and the rib cage. The appendicular skeleton is attached to the axial skeleton and consists of the bones associated with the body's appendages—the arms and legs. This includes the bones of the pectoral girdle (shoulder area), the pelvic girdle (hip area), and the arms and legs.

Axial skeleton. There are 28 bones in the skull. In adults, the bones of the cranium (part of the skull that encloses the brain) are flat and interlocking at their joints. In infants, cartilage fills the spaces between the cranial bones. Known as soft spots or fontanelles, these spaces allow the skull bones to move slightly during birth. This makes birth easier and helps prevent skull fractures. Eventually, the fontanelles are replaced by bone. In addition to protecting the brain, skull bones also support and protect the organs responsible for sight, hearing, smell, and taste.

The skull rests atop the spine, which encases and protects the spinal cord. The spine, also called the spinal column or backbone, consists of 33 stacked vertebrae, the lower ones fused. The spinal column helps to support the weight of the body and protects the spinal cord. Disks of cartilage lie between the bony vertebrae of the back and provide cushioning, like shock absorbers. The vertebrae of the spine are capable of only limited movement, such as bending and some twisting.

Twelve pair of ribs (a total of 24) extend forward from the vertebrae of the upper back. Most of the ribs (the first seven pair) attach in the front of the body via cartilage to the long, flat breastbone, or sternum. These ribs are called true ribs. The next three pair of ribs, called false ribs, do not attach to the sternum. They are connected by cartilage to the ribs above them. The lower two pair of ribs that do not attach in the front are called floating ribs. Ribs give shape to the chest and support and protect the body's major organs, such as the heart and lungs. The rib cage also provides attachment points for connective tissue, to help hold organs in place.

Appendicular skeleton. The appendicular skeleton joins with the axial skeleton at the shoulders and hips. Forming a loose attachment with the sternum is the pectoral girdle, or shoulder. Two bones, the clavicle (collar bone) and scapula (shoulder blade) form one shoulder. The major advantage to the loose attachment of the pectoral girdle is that it allows for a wide range of shoulder motions and greater overall freedom of movement.

Unlike the pectoral girdle, the pelvic girdle, or hips, is strong and dense. Each hip, left and right, consists of three fused bones—the ilium, ischium, and pubic. The pelvic girdle is bowl-shaped, with an opening at the bottom. In a pregnant woman, this bony opening is a passageway through which her baby must pass during birth. The pelvic girdle of women is generally wider than that of men, which helps to ease birth. The pelvic girdle protects the lower abdominal organs, such as the intestines, and helps supports the weight of the body above it.

The arms and legs, appendages of the body, are very similar in form. The upper arm bone, the humerus, is the long bone between the elbow and the shoulder. It connects the arm to the pectoral girdle. In the leg, the thigh bone, or femur, is the long bone between the knee and hip that connects the leg to the pelvic girdle. The humerus and femur are sturdy bones, especially the femur, which is the longest bone in the body.

At the elbow the humerus attaches to a set of parallel bones—the ulna and radius—the bones of the forearm. These bones attach to the eight small carpal bones of the wrist. The hand is made up of 19 bones.

Similarly, in the leg, the femur attaches to a set of bones of the lower leg, the fibula and tibia. The tibia, or shin bone, is larger than the fibula and forms the joint behind the patella (kneecap) with the femur. At the ankle joint, the fibula and tibia connect to the seven tarsal bones forming the ankle and heel. These, in turn, are connected to the 19 bones that make up the foot.

Bone structure

Bones may be classified according to their various traits, such as shape and texture. Four types are recognized based on shape. These are long bones, short bones, flat bones, and irregular bones. The smooth, hard outer layer of bones is called compact bone. Inside the compact bone is cancellous bone, sometimes called the bone marrow. Cancellous bone appears open and spongy, but is actually very strong, like compact bone. Together, these two types of bone produce a light, but strong, skeleton.

Bones and medicine

Even though bones are very strong, they may be broken. Fortunately, most fractures will fully heal with proper care. In children, bones often heal without a trace.

Bones are affected by poor diet and are also subject to a number of diseases and disorders. Some examples include scurvy, rickets, osteoporosis, and arthritis. Scurvy results from the lack of vitamin C. In infants, scurvy causes poor bone development. It also causes membranes surrounding the bone to bleed. Rickets is a children's disease resulting from a deficiency of vitamin D. This vitamin enables the body to absorb calcium and phosphorus. Without it, bones become soft and weak and actually bend, or bow out, under the body's weight.

The elderly, especially women who had several children in a row, sometimes suffer from osteoporosis. This condition develops when a

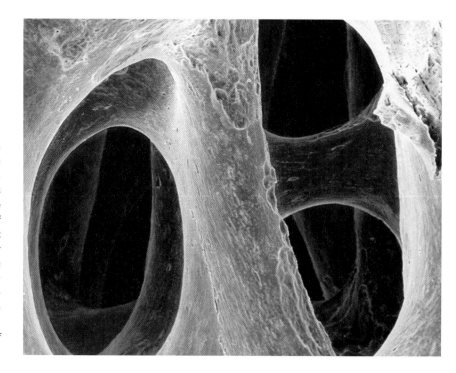

A scanning electron micrograph of normal human cancellous (spongy) bone. The shafts of long bones such as the femur are made up of two types of bone of differing densities: compact bone forms the outer region, and cancellous bone forms the core. In living cancellous bone, the cavities of the open structure contain bone marrow. *(Reproduced by permission of Photo Researchers, Inc.)*

body's calcium level is low and calcium from bones is dissolved into the blood to maintain a proper balance. Weak, brittle bones dotted with pits and pores are the result.

Another condition commonly afflicting the elderly is arthritis, an often painful inflammation of the joints. Arthritis is not, however, restricted to the elderly, as even young people may suffer from this condition. Arthritis basically involves the inflammation and deterioration of cartilage and bone at the joint surface.

[*See also* **Orthopedics**]

Slash-and-burn agriculture

Slash-and-burn agriculture refers to the process of cutting down a forest, burning the trees, and then using the cleared land to grow crops. This agricultural approach—used mainly in tropical countries—is the leading cause of tropical deforestation.

Usually, some type of slash-and-burn system is used when vast areas of tropical rain forest are converted into large-scale, industrial farms. However, slash-and-burn is more often used by individual, poor farmers who migrate to the forest frontier in search of land on which to grow food. Poor farmers operate on a smaller scale, but since there are many such people, huge areas are ultimately affected. Slash-and-burn is an often permanent conversion of the tropical rain forest into farmland, leading to severe environmental problems.

Failures of slash-and-burn agriculture

Although many species of trees and other plants grow in mature tropical rain forests, the soil of many forested sites is actually quite infertile. This poor fertility is a direct result of the climate in which tropical rain forests exist. The warm, wet tropical climate is a perfect breeding ground for bacteria and other microorganisms, which decompose or break down much of the organic matter in tropical soils. Heavy tropical rains leach (dissolve) much of the remaining organic matter or soil nutrients.

The plant species that are native to the tropical-forest ecosystem are well adapted to this soil infertility. (An ecosystem is an ecological community, including the plants, animals, and microorganisms, considered together with their environment.) They are able to absorb and conserve the small concentrations of nutrients in the soil. As a result, most of the organic nutrients in tropical rain forests are contained in the living vegetation, particularly in trees. After these trees are felled and burned, the nutrients are found in the remaining ash. However, this is a short-term phenomenon as the nutrients are quickly leached or washed away. The overall effect of slash-and-burn agriculture is a rapid decline in the fertility of the land.

Other environmental risks of tropical deforestation

Trees in tropical rain forests store huge quantities of carbon in their tissues, helping reduce the amount present in the atmosphere. The loss of tropical rain forests and the increased use of fossil fuels (such as oil and gas) have led to increased concentrations of carbon dioxide in the atmosphere—what scientists call the greenhouse effect.

Old-growth tropical rain forests are the most highly developed and diverse ecosystems on Earth. Tropical deforestation, mostly caused by slash-and-burn agriculture, is the major cause of the great wave of plant and animal extinctions that is presently plaguing Earth.

[*See also* **Forests; Rain forest**]

Slash-and-burn agriculture in Peru. *(Reproduced by permission of Photo Researchers, Inc.)*

Sleep and sleep disorders

Sleep is a normal state of decreased consciousness and lowered metabolism during which the body rests. As a natural, necessary, and daily experience for humans and most other vertebrates (animals that have a backbone or spinal column), sleep has four stages through which we cycle several times a night. A sleep disorder is any condition that interferes with our regular sleep cycle, ranging from insomnia (pronounced in-SAHM-nee-a) to narcolepsy (pronounced NAHR-ko-lehp-see).

Necessity of sleep

Although sleep is something everyone experiences everyday—the average person sleeps approximately one-third of his or her lifetime—science still has a great deal to learn about this very common phenomenon. We all recognize that sleep is a necessity and that although we can go without it for a while, it eventually becomes as important to our health and well-being as food, air, and water. We also know that when we sleep well, we seem to wake refreshed and alert, and generally feel ready to face the day. When we do not sleep well, however, we know that the chances are greater that we will feel less sharp and probably more grumpy than usual, and that everything may be a little more difficult to do. People who regularly experience a problem falling asleep or staying asleep may be suffering from some form of sleep disorder. Serious sleep disorders can wreck our personal lives, make us unproductive at work, and overall, injure the quality of our lives.

Purpose of sleep

The real nature and purpose of sleep has long puzzled scientists. Ancient humans believed that the soul left the body during sleep, and the well-known prayer that includes the words, "if I should die before I wake," tells us something about the fear we may experience when we surrender to unconsciousness every night. From a scientific standpoint, sleep was not able to be studied seriously until the twentieth century when certain instruments were invented that could actually measure brain activity. In 1929, the German psychiatrist Hans Berger (1873–1941) developed a machine called an electroencephalograph (pronounced ee-lek-tro-en-SEH-fuh-low-graf), which could pick up and record the signals produced by the brain's electrical activity. By the mid-1930s, Berger was producing a graphic picture or photograph of people's brain waves, both waking and asleep, that was called an EEG or electroencephalogram

Words to Know

Apnea: Cessation of breathing.

Circadian rhythm: The behavior of animals when influenced by the 24-hour day/night cycle.

Delta sleep: Slow-wave, stage 4 sleep that normally occurs before the onset of REM sleep.

Insomnia: Inability to go to sleep or stay asleep.

Narcolepsy: Condition characterized by brief attacks of deep sleep.

REM sleep: The period of sleep during which eyes move rapidly behind closed eyelids and when dreams most commonly occur.

(pronounced ee-lek-tro-en-SEH-fuh-low-gram). An EEG is made by placing electrode wires on a person's scalp that receive the electrical activity produced by the brain's neurons or nerve cells. Neurons in the brain receive and transmit information and are able to communicate with the rest of the body. When they are "firing" or activated, charged electrical particles are produced. It is these charges that the EEG can sense and record.

Stages of human sleep

Scientists who study the brain have discovered that certain types and levels of brain activity have their own typical patterns or register their own type of waves on an EEG. They also have come to recognize and name the certain types of waves that relate to certain types of activity. For example, when a person first closes his or her eyes after lying down, "theta" waves, or waves that have a certain number of cycles per second, are produced. As a person falls into deeper stages of sleep, the waves become slower. Although they do not know exactly why this happens, scientists do know that most vertebrates pass through two distinct types of sleep, and that humans have four separate levels of sleep. In Stage I we have just fallen asleep, usually after about fifteen minutes, and we have entered a light, dozing sleep. Here we show irregular and fairly fast theta waves. Stage II is the first true stage of sleep, and our EEG registers "spindle waves" in bursts. Stage III marks the beginning of deep sleep, and theta waves that are slowed-down appear. Stage IV is our deepest sleep and has the slowest waves of all, sometimes called delta waves. This progression from stages one to four takes about one hour, and then the cycle reverses itself, going backwards to Stage I. This entire cycle repeats itself three or four times during the night.

REM sleep

At the end of the first cycle, each time a person reenters Stage I, he or she begins an interesting sleep stage called Rapid Eye Movement or REM sleep. It is during this stage that our dreaming occurs, and even though this is a stage of light sleep, most people are difficult to awaken when in REM sleep. Our bodies are also very active during REM, and besides our eyes moving side to side, we usually toss and turn quite a bit. of sleep a night. Most adults average around seven and a half hours of sleep a night, although studies have shown that some people need as little as five or six hours. Regardless, everyone needs their REM sleep. We spend about three-fourths of a night in non-REM sleep and one-fourth dreaming in REM sleep. Amazingly, the brain waves registered during REM are almost the same as those when we are awake.

How much sleep?

Our sleep patterns change as we age, and infants sleep far longer and deeper than adults. Newborns may sleep as much as seventeen hours a day, while five-year-olds about twelve hours a night. Teenagers need about nine and a half hours a night, although they seldom get that much. For some reason, many people experience the best and most satisfying sleep of their lives during the middle teen years. Some very old adults need only five or six hours a night.

Insomnia

Although sleep is something that is common to us all, many people—as many as 30 million Americans—suffer from some sort of sleep disorder or problem. Insomnia or difficulty falling or staying asleep is the most common disorder. While everyone will experience this at some time, if you regularly have trouble getting to sleep or staying asleep and feel next-day sleepiness and difficulty concentrating, you probably have insomnia. Some of the causes of insomnia are psychological factors like stress. Your lifestyle itself may cause a different kind of stress if you regularly work or party very late or drink alcohol or beverages with caffeine. An unsettling environment can be a factor, as can physical problems that cause pain. Certain medications can also cause sleeping problems. A simple description of insomnia is that it happens when the part of the brain used for thinking does not turn off.

Narcolepsy

Probably the most serious sleeping disorder is a chronic brain disorder called narcolepsy (pronounced nar-ka-LEP-see). It affects some 200,000 Americans and is recognized primarily by a sudden, almost uncontrollable need to sleep that can occur at any time. Narcoleptics may also experience sudden muscle weakness, a feeling of being paralyzed, and even especially frightening nightmares and hallucinations. It can be brought on by being bored but also by being surprised, angry, or suddenly upset. The poor narcoleptic always feels tired during the day. This difficult condition is a genetic disorder, meaning that it runs in families. It is managed with stimulant-type drugs.

Many hospitals and universities run sleep labs where they monitor the sleeping patterns of people with varying sleep disorders. *(Reproduced by permission of Photo Researchers, Inc.)*

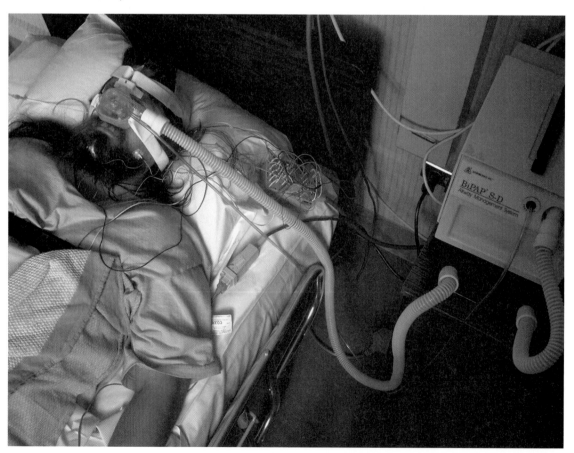

Sleep apnea

Sleep apnea (pronounced AP-knee-ah) sounds like a funny condition when it is described, except it can be potentially very serious. Sufferers from sleep apnea can develop high blood pressure and even risk heart damage. This condition occurs most often in middle-aged men who literally stop breathing while asleep. When this happens, they usually snort or snore and gasp for breath, waking themselves up. This can happen as often as two hundred times a night, obviously wrecking any chance of a good night's sleep and leading to daytime sleepiness, headaches, irritability, and even learning and memory problems. Most cases are caused by some sort of abnormality in the nose, throat, or other part of the airway. Some sufferers can wear a masklike device over their nose whose regulated pressure prevents their throat from collapsing during sleep. Others may need surgery.

Other sleep disorders

There are several other types of sleep disorders, some serious and some simply bothersome. Some people have Restless Leg Syndrome (RLS), in which they experience terribly uncomfortable sensations in their legs and have to move, stretch, or rub their legs all the time. This naturally disturbs their sleep. This condition is sometimes treated with drugs. Others have Periodic Limb Movement (PLM), in which their legs (and sometimes their arms) periodically twitch and jerk, sometimes for as long as several hours. Like RLS, the cause is unknown.

Many people who work or are active during the night and try to sleep during the day experience difficulty sleeping. This is called a disruption of one's circadian (pronounced sir-KAY-dee-an) rhythm. This means that the body's internal clock is out of sync with the twenty-four-hour day. The "jet lag" we feel after changing time zones is a temporary example of such a disorder. Finally, many people at some time have experienced other minor disorders, such as sleepwalking, "night terrors," teeth grinding, and talking in one's sleep.

Although scientists are still not sure exactly what the function of sleep is—whether the brain is "housekeeping" and reorganizing the information it took in during the day or simply conserving its energy—they do know that it provides all-important rest to the mind and body, and that rest is essential to good health. Therefore, sleep is not simply a "time out" from business. It is a necessary time of restoration. This is demonstrated by the ill effects experienced by those who suffer from a sleep disorder.

Smell

Smell, called olfaction, is the ability of an organism to sense and identify a substance by detecting tiny amounts of the substance that evaporate and produce an odor. Smell is the most important sense for most organisms. Many species use their sense of smell to locate prey, navigate, recognize and communicate with others of their species, and mark territory.

The sense of smell differs from most other senses (sight, hearing, taste, and touch) in its directness. We actually smell microscopic bits of a substance that have evaporated and made their way to the olfactory epithelium, a section of the mucous membrane in the roof of the nasal

The process by which olfactory information is transmitted to the brain. (Reproduced by permission of The Gale Group.)

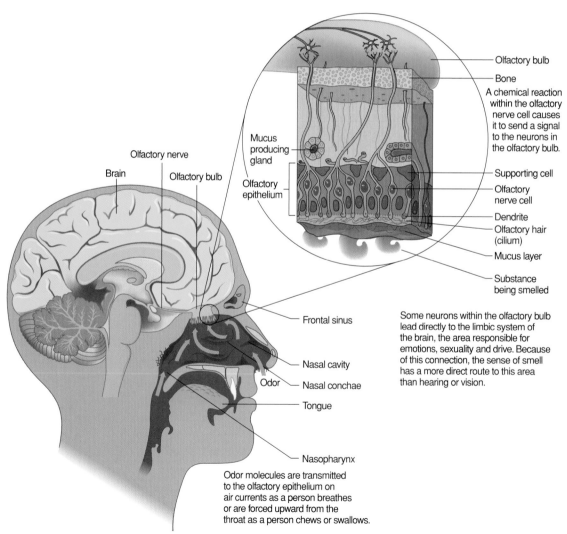

Olfactory bulb

Bone

A chemical reaction within the olfactory nerve cell causes it to send a signal to the neurons in the olfactory bulb.

Mucus producing gland

Olfactory nerve

Brain

Olfactory bulb

Olfactory epithelium

Supporting cell

Olfactory nerve cell

Dendrite

Olfactory hair (cilium)

Mucus layer

Substance being smelled

Frontal sinus

Some neurons within the olfactory bulb lead directly to the limbic system of the brain, the area responsible for emotions, sexuality and drive. Because of this connection, the sense of smell has a more direct route to this area than hearing or vision.

Nasal cavity

Odor

Nasal conchae

Tongue

Nasopharynx

Odor molecules are transmitted to the olfactory epithelium on air currents as a person breathes or are forced upward from the throat as a person chews or swallows.

Words to Know

Olfactory bulb: The primitive part of the brain that first processes olfactory information.

Olfactory epithelium: The patch of mucous membrane at the top of the nasal cavity that contains the olfactory nerve cells.

Olfactory nerve cell: A cell in the olfactory epithelium that detects odors and transmits the information to the brain.

Pheromone: Scent molecules released by animals that affect the behavior of organisms of the same species.

cavity of the nose. The olfactory epithelium contains millions of odor-sensitive olfactory nerve cells that are connected to the olfactory nerves. Hairlike fibers on the end of each olfactory cell react to an odor by stimulating the olfactory cells to send a signal along the olfactory nerve to the brain, which interprets the signal as a specific smell.

Human versus animal smell

There is no doubt that many animals have a sense of smell far superior to that of humans. Most vertebrates (animals with backbones) have many more olfactory nerve cells than humans. This probably gives them much more sensitivity to odors. Also, the structure in the brain that processes odors (called the olfactory bulb) takes up a much larger part of the brain in animals than in humans. Thus, animals have a greater ability to process and analyze different odors. This is why humans use dogs to find lost persons, hidden drugs, and explosives—although research on "artificial noses" that can detect scent even more reliably than dogs continues.

Still, the human nose is capable of detecting over 10,000 different odors, even some that occur in extremely minute amounts in the air. Many researchers are considering whether smell does not play a greater role in human behavior and biology than has been previously thought. For instance, research has shown that human mothers can smell the difference between clothes worn by their baby and those worn by another baby only days after the child's birth.

Scientists are only beginning to understand the role that smell plays in animal—and human—behavior. For example, animals release chemicals called pheromones to communicate danger, defend themselves against predators, mark territory, and attract mates. Some researchers have suggested that humans also may release pheromones that play a role in sexual attraction and mating—although this hypothesis has not been proven.

Current research

Olfactory nerve cells are the only nerve cells arising from the central nervous system that can regenerate (be formed again). Some researchers hope that studying regeneration in olfactory nerve cells or even transplanting them elsewhere in the body can lead to treatments for spine and brain damage that is currently irreversible.

Snakes

Snakes are limbless reptiles with long, cylindrical bodies, scaly skin, lidless eyes, and a forked tongue. Most species are not poisonous, some are mildly poisonous, and others produce a deadly poison. The term venom is commonly used to describe the poison produced by a snake.

All snakes are carnivores (meat-eaters) and cold blooded, meaning their body temperature is determined by the environment rather than being internally regulated. For this reason, snakes are found mainly in tropical and temperate regions, and are absent in cold climate zones.

Types of snakes

The 2,700 species of snakes fall into four superfamilies: Boidae (boas, anacondas, and pythons), Elapidae (cobras, coral snakes, mambas, and kraits), Colubridae (king snakes, water snakes, garter snakes, black snakes, and adders, to name only a few) and Viperidae (true vipers and pit vipers).

Members of the Boidae family are among the most primitive of all snakes. They are constrictors that kill their prey by squeezing it to death. Some of the largest snakes are members of this family. Some anacondas, for example, have been known to grow to more than 11 meters (37 feet) in length.

Snakes in the Elapidae family have grooved or hollow fangs in the front of the mouth. The bases of the fangs are connected to the venom gland. Venom is injected when the victim is bitten. Members of this fam-

Words to Know

Carnivore: A flesh-eating animal.

Jacobson's organs: Chemical sensors located on the roof of the mouth of a snake used to detect chemical "smells."

Molt: To shed an outer layer of skin at regular intervals.

Venom: A poison produced by a snake.

ily range in size from the tiny elapids, which may be no more than a few centimeters long, to the feared taipan, which may grow to nearly four meters (12 feet) in length.

The Colubridae family is huge, with more than 1,400 species, and includes the majority of living species. Most colubrids are harmless, but a few are extremely dangerous. Examples are the rear-fanged snakes, such as the African boomslang or the crown snake. These snakes do not release their poison through hollow fangs. Instead, they inject poison by chewing their prey after it is in their mouth.

Members of the Viperidae family are among the most dangerous of all snakes. They include in addition to the vipers themselves the rattlesnake, fer-de-lance, and bushmaster. Most members of the family have a wedge-shaped head that people have come to associate with poisonous snakes.

Anatomy and physiology

Snakes have extremely poor sight and hearing. They detect their prey primarily by means of vibrations, heat, and chemical signals they detect with their other senses. For example, a snake's flicking, forked tongue acts as a chemical collector, drawing chemical "smells" into the mouth. Those smells are then analyzed by two chemical sensors known as Jacobson's organs on the roof of its mouth. This mechanism also allows male snakes to detect females in the reproductive state.

Another mechanism used by snakes to detect prey is a set of tiny pits or hollows that certain kinds of vipers have on the side or top of their heads. These pits can detect the body heat of prey at considerable distances.

Contrary to popular belief, snakes are not slimy. The scales that cover their bodies are dry but glistening, giving a sheen that offers an appearance of wetness. Scales protect the snake's body from friction and dehydration. They also aid its movement by gripping the surface while powerful muscles propel the body forward, usually with a horizontal waving motion. This method of movement means that snakes cannot move backward.

Instead of eyelids, the eyes of snakes are covered and protected by clear scales. Several times a year, snakes molt, shedding their skin in one complete piece by rubbing against a rough surface.

Snakes' teeth do not allow them to chew and break up the bodies of their prey. Instead, they usually swallow their prey whole. Special ligaments in the snake's hinged jaw permit its mouth to open to as much as a 150-degree angle. Thus, the snake can swallow animals many times larger than the size of its own head. The largest recorded feast was a 130-pound (59-kilogram) antelope swallowed by an African rock python.

Snakes' teeth face inward and prevent the prey from escaping. The snake's strong jaw and throat muscles work the food down the esophagus and into the stomach, where digestion begins. Digestion time differs, and is influenced by temperature. In one instance, a captive python at a room temperature of 30°C (87°F) digested a rabbit in four days. At cooler temperatures (18°C; 64°F), however, digestion took more than two weeks.

A timber rattlesnake consuming a mouse. (Reproduced by permission of JLM Visuals.)

The interval between meals also varies. Some snakes go weeks or even months without food. In temperate climates, snakes may fast and hibernate during the winter months. Pregnant females may hibernate and fast seven months, while both sexes fast before shedding.

Hunting and defense

The coloring of a snake's skin scales provides an excellent camouflage from predators and prey. Tree snakes can have a color as green as any leaf in the forest; ground snakes are as brown or dusty grey as the earth and rocks; and sea snakes are dark above and light beneath. Some snakes are brightly colored with vivid patterns that warn potential predators to stay away. An example is the highly venomous coral snake, which has orange, black, and white rings.

Snakes attack only when hungry or threatened. When frightened, they tend to flee. If there is no time for flight, or if snakes are cornered or antagonized, they strike. Venomous snakes have two fangs in the upper jaw that penetrate the flesh of their prey. Poison glands then pump venom through grooves inside the fangs into the prey. Some species of snake inject their prey with toxin and wait until the animal is no longer capable of struggling before eating it. Snake venom is purely a feeding aid, serving both to subdue the prey and to aid in its digestion before it is swallowed.

Nonvenomous constrictors, such as boas, pythons, and anacondas, first snatch their prey in their jaws. Then, with lightning speed, they coil their bodies around the animal, squeezing its thorax to prevent breathing. Amazingly, the prey's bones remain unbroken during this process.

Snakes and humans

Snakes have fascinated and frightened humans for thousands of years. Some cultures still worship snakes, seeing them as creators and protectors. Other cultures fear snakes as devils and symbols of death.

In many ways, snakes serve a valuable function for human societies. They prey on animals, such as rats and mice, that we often regard as pests. Many people enjoy keeping snakes as pets also.

On the other hand, many people have a terrible fear of these reptiles. They may believe that the only good snake is a dead snake. Unfortunately, this attitude leads to the death of many harmless snakes. Yet, as much as most humans fear snakes, snakes fear humans more. Certainly, some snakes can kill a human in a matter of minutes, and no snake should be handled unless positively identified as harmless. However, the estimated risk of venomous snakebites to humans in the United States is 20 times less than being struck by lightning. Overall, a well-educated, healthy respect for snakes would benefit both humans and snakes.

[See also **Reptiles**]

Soaps and detergents

A detergent is a cleaning agent. Detergents can be classified into one of two general categories: natural soaps (or just soaps) and synthetic detergents (or syndets). Both soaps and syndets have many similarities, particularly with regard to their molecular structures and the way they clean objects.

The structure of soaps and detergents

Both soaps and syndets consist of very long molecules. A model of such molecules is shown below:

$$CH_3CH_2CH_2CH_2CH_2CH_2CH_2CH_2CH_2CH_2CH_2CH_2CH_2CH_2CH_2CHCOO^-, Na^+$$

The characteristic of all such molecules is that they have very different ends. The left end of the above molecule is said to be hydrophobic, meaning it "hates water." That end of the molecule is attracted by fats and oils, but not by water. The right end of the molecule above is said to be hydrophilic, meaning it "loves water." That end of the molecule is attracted by water but not by fats and oils.

Most of the dirt that collects on clothing, dishes, and our bodies is surrounded by a thin layer of oil. Simply washing an object with water is not a very effective way of getting the object clean because oil and water do not mix with each other.

But suppose that a detergent, either a soap or a syndet, is added to the wash water. In that case, detergent molecules line up with one end attached to the oily dirt and the other end attached to water molecules. When the object is scrubbed or agitated, the oil-covered dirt attached to detergent molecules, which are also attached to water molecules, is removed from clothing, dishes, or human skin. The dirt-detergent-water combination can then disappear down the drain.

Soaps

No one knows exactly when soap was discovered. It was apparently used by the Phoenicians as early as the sixth century B.C. Modern methods of soapmaking were not perfected, however, until late in the eighteenth century. In 1790, French chemist Nicholas Leblanc (1742–1806) invented a process for making caustic soda (sodium hydroxide) from common table salt (sodium chloride). His invention made it possible to manufacture soap inexpensively from ordinary raw materials.

Soap is made by heating together fats or oils with water solutions of sodium hydroxide (lye). Molecules of fats and oils are very long molecules, like the one shown above. They do not have the charged group at the end of the molecule ($—COO^-$, Na^+) as shown in that structure, however. The charged group is obtained from the sodium hydroxide with which the fat or oil is mixed.

Anyone can make his or her own soap simply by boiling a fat and lye together in a metal pot. The soap produced, however, would normally not be very pleasant to use. It would probably contain some left-over lye, which is very harsh. Washing with lye soap gets things clean but can be very damaging to human skin.

Today, soaps contain a number of ingredients to make them more pleasant to use. These ingredients include perfumes and coloring agents. Soaps may also be whipped into a lather when they are still liquid, to make them float; pressed into very hard bars, to make them last longer; or treated in other ways to give them special properties.

Synthetic detergents

Soap is one of the greatest chemical products ever invented by humans. It is highly effective in getting objects clean and in killing bacteria. But soap also has its disadvantages. Perhaps the most important of these disadvantages is its tendency to form precipitates in hard water.

Hard water gets its name because of the fact that it is hard to make suds when trying to use soap in it. Perhaps you have seen the grayish scum that forms in a bathtub or a wash basin after you've taken a bath or washed some clothes in well water. The scum is a precipitate formed when soap reacts with the chemicals that make water hard.

Washing with soap in hard water is a wasteful activity. The first thing that happens when you add soap to hard water is that the soap reacts with chemicals to form scum. In a way, you are just throwing away the first batch of soap you add because it can not be used to clean anything. Once all the chemicals in hard water are used up, then any additional soap can be used for cleaning something.

Syndets do not have this problem. When a syndet is added to hard water, no precipitate is formed. The syndet is ready to go to work immediately to start cleaning something.

The discovery of syndets in the 1940s had, therefore, a very dramatic effect on the soap market. In 1940, more than three billion pounds of soap were manufactured in the United States. Five years later, that number had risen to almost four billion pounds. In the same year, the first syndets began to appear on the market. After 1945, the amount of soap produced began to fall, while the amount of syndets began to increase. By 1970, about one billion pounds of soap was produced in the United States compared to nearly six billion pounds of syndets.

As with soaps, syndets are always a mixture of substances that includes more than the cleaning agent itself. These additives include brighteners, bleaching agents, fillers, "builders," and perfumes and coloring agents.

[*See also* **Alkali metals**]

Soil

Soil, which covers most of the land surface of Earth, is a complex mixture of weathered rock debris and partially decayed organic (plant and animal) matter. Soil not only supports a huge number of organisms below its surface—bacteria, fungi, worms, insects, and small mammals—but it is essential to all life on the planet. Soil provides a medium in which plants can grow, supporting their roots and providing them with water, oxygen, and other nutrients for growth.

Soil now covers Earth in depths from a few inches to several feet. Soils began to form billions of years ago as rain washed minerals out of the molten rocks that were cooling on the planet's surface. The rains leached or dissolved potassium, calcium, and magnesium—minerals essential for plant growth—from the rocks onto the surface. This loose mineral matter or parent material was then scattered over Earth by wind, water, or glacial ice, creating the conditions in which very simple plants could evolve. Plant life eventually spread and flourished.

As these early plants died, they left behind organic residues. Animals, bacteria, and fungi fed on this organic matter, breaking it down further and enriching the parent material with nutrients and energy for more complex plant growth. Over time, more and more organic matter mixed with the parent material, a process that continues to this day.

Soil is generally composed of 50 percent solid material and 50 percent space. About 90 percent of the solid portion of soil is composed of

Words to Know

Bedrock: Solid layer of rock lying beneath Earth's surface.

Clay: Portion of soil comprising the smallest soil particles.

Horizons: Layers of soil that have built up over time and lie parallel to the surface of Earth.

Humus: Fragrant, spongy, nutrient-rich material resulting from the decomposition of organic matter.

Leaching: Downward movement through soil of chemical substances dissolved in water.

Loam: Soil that contains a balance of fine clay, medium-sized silt, and coarse sand particles.

Organic matter: Remains, residues, or waste products of any living organism.

Parent material: Loose mineral matter scattered over Earth by wind, water, or glacial ice or weathered in place from rocks.

Sand: Granular portion of soil composed of the largest soil particles.

Silt: Medium-sized soil particles.

Soil profile: Combined soil horizons or layers.

Topsoil: Uppermost layer of soil that contains high levels of organic matter.

tiny bits of rock and minerals. These solid particles range in size from fine clay to mid-range silt to relatively large, coarse sand. The remaining 10 percent is made up of organic matter—living plant roots and plant and animal remains, residue, or waste products.

The proportion of solid material in soil determines the amount of oxygen, water, and nutrients that will be available for plants. Since smaller particles stick together when wet, soil with a lot of clay holds water well, but drains poorly. Clay particles also pack together tightly, allowing for little air space. As a result, plant roots suffer from a lack of oxygen. Sand particles do not hold water or nutrients well. The best soil for plant growth is one in which all three types of particles—clay, silt, and sand—are in balance. Such a soil is called loam.

Soil horizons and profile

Once soil has developed, it is composed of horizontal layers with differing physical or chemical characteristics and varying thickness and color. These layers, called horizons, each represent a distinct soil that has built up over a long time period. The layers together form the soil profile. Soil scientists have created many different designations for different types of soil horizons. The most basic soil layers are the A, B, and C horizons.

The A horizon, the top layer, includes topsoil. The A horizon generally contains organic matter mixed with soil particles of sand, silt, and

The climate in different regions can affect the soil, sometimes molding it into strange shapes or geologic formations. *(Reproduced by permission of Field Mark Publications.)*

clay. The amount of organic matter varies widely from region to region. In mountainous areas, organic matter is likely to make up only a small portion of the soil, from 1 to 6 percent. In low wet areas, organic matter may account for as much as 90 percent of soil content. Because it contains organic matter, the A horizon is generally darker in color than the deeper layers. The surface of the A layer is sometimes covered with a very thin layer of loose organic debris.

Below the A layer is the subsoil, the B horizon. This layer usually contains high levels of clay, minerals, and other inorganic compounds as water forced down by gravity through the A horizon carries these particles into the B horizon. This natural process is called leaching.

The A and B horizons lie atop the C horizon, which is found far enough below the surface that it contains little organic matter. Fragmented rocks and small stones make up most of the C horizon. Beneath this horizon lies bedrock, the solid layer of rock that lies underneath all soil.

Life in the soil

Soils teem with life. In fact, more creatures live below the surface of Earth than above. Among these soil dwellers are bacteria, fungi, and algae, which exist in vast numbers (bacteria are the most abundant). Three-hundredths of an ounce (one gram) of soil may contain from several hundred million to a few billion microorganisms. These microscopic organisms feed on plant and animal remains, breaking them down into humus, the dark, crumbly organic component of soil present in the A horizon. Humus cannot be broken down any further by microorganisms in the soil. It is a very important aspect of soil quality. Humus holds water like a sponge, serves as a reservoir for plant nutrients, and makes soil particles clump together, helping to aerate the soil.

Ants abound in soils. They create mazes of tunnels and construct mounds, mixing soils and bringing up subsurface soils in the process. They also gather vegetation into their mounds, which become rich in organic matter as a result. By burrowing and recolonizing, ants can eventually rework and fertilize the soil covering an entire prairie.

Earthworms burrow through soils, mixing organic material with minerals as they go and aerating the soil. Some earthworms pull leaves from the forest floor into their burrows (called middens), enriching the soil. Almost 4,000 worms can inhabit an acre of soil. Their burrowing can bring 7 to 18 tons of soil to the surface annually.

Larger animals inhabit soils, including moles, which tunnel just below the surface eating earthworms, grubs, and plant roots. In doing so, they loosen the soil and make it more porous. Mice also burrow, as do ground squirrels, marmots, and prairie dogs. All bring tons of subsoil material to the surface. These animals all prefer dry areas, so the soils they unearth are often sandy and gravelly.

Soil erosion

Erosion is any process that transports soil from one place to another. At naturally occurring rates, land typically loses about 1 inch (2.5 centimeters) of topsoil in 100 to 250 years. A tolerable rate of soil erosion is considered to be 48 to 80 pounds of soil per acre (55 to 91 kilograms per hectare) each year. Weathering processes that produce soil from rock can replace soil at this rate. However, cultivation, construction, and other human activities have increased the rate of soil erosion. Some parts of North America are losing as much as 18 tons of soil per acre (40 metric ton per hectare) per year.

The surface layer of soil (topsoil) provides most of the nutrients needed by plants. Because most erosion occurs on the surface of the soil, this vital layer is the most susceptible to being lost. The fertilizers and pesticides in some eroded soils may also pollute rivers and lakes. Eroded soil damages dams and culverts, fisheries, and reservoirs when it accumulates in those structures as sediment.

[*See also* **Erosion**]

Solar system

Our solar system consists of the Sun and all of its orbiting objects. These objects include the planets with their rings and moons, asteroids, comets, meteors and meteorites, and particles of dust and debris.

The Sun, which keeps these objects in orbit with its gravitational field, alone accounts for about 99.8 percent of the mass of the solar system. Jupiter, the largest planet, represents another 0.1 percent of the mass. Everything else in the solar system together makes up the remaining 0.1 percent.

The average distance between the Sun and Pluto, the farthest planet, is about 3.66 billion miles (5.89 billion kilometers). Incorporating the entire space within the orbit of Pluto, the area encompassed by the solar system is 41.85 billion square miles (108.4 billion square kilometers). Our solar system seems quite insignificant, however, when considered in the

Words to Know

Light-year: Distance light travels in one year in the vacuum of space, roughly 5.9 trillion miles (9.5 trillion kilometers).

Nuclear fusion: Merging of two hydrogen nuclei into one helium nucleus, releasing a tremendous amount of energy in the process.

Oort cloud: Region of space beyond the solar system that theoretically contains about one trillion inactive comets.

Planetesimals: Ancient chunks of matter that originated with the formation of the solar system but never came together to form a planet.

Protoplanet: Earliest form of a planet, plus its moons, formed by the combination of planetesimals.

Solar wind: Electrically charged subatomic particles that flow out from the Sun.

Supernova: Explosion of a massive star at the end of its lifetime, causing it to shine more brightly than the rest of the stars in the galaxy put together.

context of the more than 100 billion stars in our galaxy, the Milky Way, and the estimated 50 billion galaxies in the universe.

Planets

A planet is defined as a body that orbits a star (in our case the Sun) and produces no light of its own, but reflects the light of its controlling star. At present, scientists know of nine planets in the solar system. They are grouped into three categories: the solid, terrestrial planets; the giant, gaseous (also known as Jovian) planets; and Pluto.

The terrestrial planets, the first group closest to the Sun, consists of Mercury, Venus, Earth, and Mars. The atmospheres of these planets contain (in varying amounts) nitrogen, carbon dioxide, oxygen, water, and argon.

The Jovian planets, father from the Sun, consist of Jupiter, Saturn, Uranus, and Neptune. The light gases hydrogen and helium make up almost 100 percent of the thick atmospheres of these planets. Another difference between the giant planets and the terrestrial planets is the existence of ring systems. Although the rings around Saturn are the most spectacular and the only ones visible from Earth, Jupiter, Uranus, and Neptune do have rings.

On the basis of distance from the Sun, Pluto might be considered a Jovian planet, but its size places it in the terrestrial group. The major component of its thin atmosphere is probably methane, which exists in a frozen state for much of the planet's inclined orbit around the Sun.

Moons

A moon is any natural satellite (as opposed to a human-made satellite) that orbits a planet. Seven of the planets in the solar system—Earth, Mars, Jupiter, Saturn, Uranus, Neptune, and Pluto—have moons, which total 61. Although moons do not orbit the Sun independently, they are still considered members of the solar system.

Asteroids

Asteroids are relatively small chunks of rock that orbit the Sun. Except for their small size, they are similar to planets. For this reason, they are often referred to as minor planets. Scientists believe that asteroids are

A schematic of the present-day solar system, showing the position of the planets' orbits around the Sun, comparative sizes (to each other, not the Sun), the direction in which they rotate, and the tilt of their axes. (Reproduced by permission of The Gale Group.)

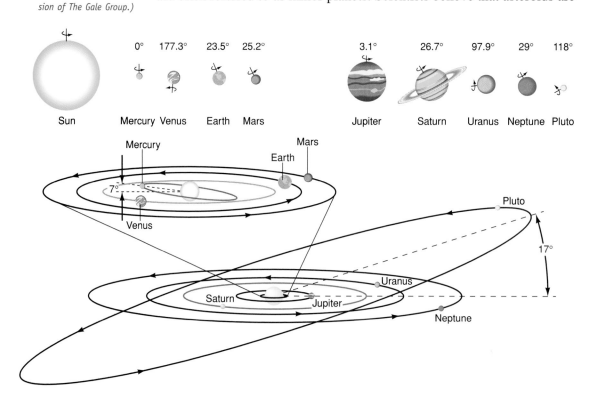

ancient pieces of matter that were created with the formation of the solar system but never came together to form a planet. An estimated one million asteroids may exist in the solar system. About 95 percent of all asteroids occupy a band of space between the orbits of Mars and Jupiter. The largest of the asteroids, named Ceres, is 580 miles (940 kilometers) in diameter, while the smallest one measured to date is only 33 feet (10 meters) in diameter.

Comets

Comets are made of dust and rocky material mixed with frozen methane, ammonia, and water. A comet speeds around the Sun on an elongated orbit. It consists of a nucleus, a head, and a gaseous tail. The tail forms when some of the comet melts as it nears the Sun and the melted material is swept back by the solar wind. Scientists believe comets originate on the edge of the solar system in an area called the Oort cloud. This space is occupied by trillions of inactive comets, which remain there until a passing gas cloud or star jolts one into orbit around the Sun.

The origin of the solar system

Over time, there have been various theories put forth as to the origin of the solar system. Most of these have since been disproved and discarded. Today the theory scientists consider most likely to be correct is a modified version of the nebular hypothesis first suggested in 1755 by German philosopher Immanuel Kant and later advanced by French mathematician Pierre-Simon Laplace.

The modern solar nebula hypothesis states that the Sun and planets formed 4.6 billion years ago from the solar nebula—a cloud of interstellar gas and dust. Due to the mutual gravitational attraction of the material in the nebula, and possibly triggered by shock waves from a nearby supernova, the nebula eventually collapsed in on itself.

As the nebula contracted, it spun increasingly rapidly, leading to frequent collisions between dust grains. These grains stuck together to form pebbles, then boulders, and then planetesimals. Solid particles as well as gas continued to stick to these planetesimals (in what's known as the accretion theory), eventually forming protoplanets, or planets in their early stages.

As the nebula continued to condense, the temperature at its core rose to the point where nuclear fusion reactions began, forming the Sun. The protoplanets spinning around the developing Sun formed the planets.

Other solar systems?

Evidence has come to light suggesting that ours may not be the only solar system in the galaxy. In late 1995 and early 1996, three new planets were found, ranging in distance from 35 to 40 light-years from Earth. The first planet, discovered by Swiss astronomers Michel Mayor and Didier Queloz, orbits a star in the constellation Pegasus. The next two planets were discovered by American astronomers Geoffrey Marcy and R. Paul Butler. One is in the constellation Virgo and the other is in Ursa Major. Other planetary discoveries soon followed, and by spring 2001, astronomers had found evidence of 63 known planets outside our solar system.

Of perhaps greater importance to the study of solar systems was the announcement in 1999 that astronomers had discovered the first planetary system outside of our own. They detected three planets circling the star Upsilon Andromedae, some forty-four light-years away. Two of the three planets are at least twice as massive as Jupiter, and astronomers sus-

An artist's conception of the formation of the solar system. The terrestrial planets received the same combination of gases present in the solar nebula (gas cloud), but once formed, each planet's atmosphere evolved as a result of its relative gravity and distance from the Sun. (Reproduced by permission of Photo Researchers, Inc.)

pect they are huge spheres of gas without a solid surface. The innermost planet lies extremely close to Upsilon Andromedae—about one-eighth the distance at which Mercury circles the Sun.

The discovery of two more planetary systems in the universe was announced by astronomers in early 2001. Each is different from the other and from our solar system. In one, a star like our Sun is orbited by a massive planet and an even larger object seventeen times the size of Jupiter. According to astronomers, this large object could be a dim, failed star or an astronomical object that simply has not been seen before. In the second system, a small star is orbited by two planets of more normal size. Their orbits around the star, however, puzzle astronomers: the inner planet orbits almost twice as fast as the outer planet. With these discoveries at the beginning of the twenty-first century, astronomers may have to redefine what a normal planetary system is in the universe.

[*See also* **Asteroid; Comet; Cosmology; Earth; Extrasolar planet; Mars; Jupiter; Mercury; Meteors and meteorites; Neptune; Orbit; Pluto; Saturn; Sun; Uranus; Venus**]

Solution

A solution is a homogeneous mixture of two or more substances. The term homogeneous means "the same throughout." For example, suppose that you make a solution of sugar in water. If you were to take a drop of the sugar solution from anywhere in the solution, it would always have the same composition.

Terminology

A number of specialized terms are used in talking about solutions. The solvent in a solution is the substance that does the dissolving. The solute is the substance that is dissolved. In the sugar solution described above, the water is the solvent and the sugar is the solute.

Although that definition is neat, it does not always make a lot of sense. For example, one can make a solution of two gases. In fact, the air around us is a solution consisting of oxygen, nitrogen, argon, carbon dioxide, and other gases. In this case, it is difficult to say which gas "does the dissolving" and which gas (or gases) "is dissolved."

An alternative method of defining solvent and solute is to say that the component of the solution present in the largest amount is the solvent

▼ Words to Know

Concentration: The amount of a substance (solute) present in a given volume of solvent or solution.

Homogeneous: The same throughout.

Miscibility: The extent to which some substance will mix with some other substance.

Saturated: In referring to solutions, a solution that contains the maximum amount of solute for a given amount of solvent at a given temperature.

Solubility: The tendency of a substance to dissolve in some other substance.

Solute: The substance that is "dissolved" or that exists in the least amount in a solution.

Solvent: The substance that "does the dissolving" or that exists in the largest amount in a solution.

Supersaturated: In referring to solutions, a solution that contains more than the maximum amount of solvent that can normally be dissolved in a given amount of solvent at a given temperature.

Unsaturated: In referring to solutions, a solution that contains less than the maximum amount of solvent that can be dissolved in a given amount of solvent at a given temperature.

while the components present in lesser amounts are solute. According to that definition, nitrogen is the solvent in atmospheric air because it is present in the largest amount. Oxygen, argon, carbon dioxide, and other gases, then, are the solutes.

The term miscible is often used to describe how well two substances—generally, two liquids—mix with each other. For example, if you try to mix oil with water, you will find that the two do not mix very well at all. They are said to be immiscible—incapable of mixing. In contrast, ethyl alcohol and water are completely miscible because they mix with each other in all proportions.

Solubility is a term similar to miscibility but more exact. The solubility of a substance is the amount of the substance that will dissolve in a given amount of solvent. For example, the solubility of sugar in water is approximately 90 grams of sugar per 100 grams of water. That statement means that one can dissolve up to 90 grams of sugar in 100 grams of water.

The solubility of a substance is dependent on the temperature. The statement in the previous paragraph, for example, should have been that 90 grams of sugar will dissolve in 100 grams of water at some specific temperature. That temperature happens to be 0°C.

Generally speaking, the solubility of substances increases with temperature. The graph in Figure 1 illustrates this point. Notice that the solubility of sugar increases to a little over 100 grams per 100 grams of water at 25°C and to 130 grams per 100 grams of water at 50°C.

An important exception to this rule concerns gases. All gases become less soluble in water as the temperature increases.

Concentration of solutions

Solutions are mixtures whose composition can vary widely. One can make a water solution of sodium chloride by dissolving 1 gram of sodium chloride in 100 grams of water; 5 grams in 100 grams of water; 10 grams in 100 grams of water; and so on. The amount of solute for any given amount of solvent is defined as the concentration of the solution.

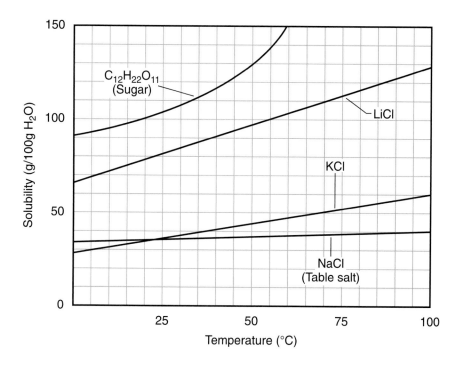

Figure 1. (Reproduced by permission of The Gale Group.)

One way of expressing the concentration of a solution is with the terms dilute and concentrated. These terms are not very specific. For example, a solution containing 1 gram of sodium chloride in 100 grams of water and a second solution containing 2 grams of sodium chloride in 100 grams of water are both dilute. But the term is appropriate because, at room temperature, nearly 40 grams of sodium chloride can be dissolved in 100 grams of water. Thus, a solution containing 35 grams of sodium chloride in 100 grams of water could be called a concentrated solution.

Solutions can also be classified as saturated, unsaturated, or supersaturated. A saturated solution is one that holds all the solute it possibly can at any given temperature. For example, the solubility of sodium chloride in water is 37 grams per 100 grams of water. If you make a solution containing 37 grams of sodium chloride in 100 grams of water, the solution is said to be saturated; it can't hold any more sodium chloride.

Any solution containing less than the maximum possible amount of solute is said to be unsaturated. A solution with 5 grams of sodium chloride (or 10 grams or 20 grams or 30 grams) in 100 grams of water is unsaturated.

Finally, supersaturated solutions are also possible. As bizarre as it sounds, a supersaturated solution is one that holds more solute than is possible at some given temperature. The way to make a supersaturated solution is to make a saturated solution at some higher temperature and then let the solution cool very carefully.

For example, one could make a saturated solution of sugar in water at 50°C by adding 130 grams of sugar to 100 grams of water. That solution would be saturated. But then, one could allow the solution to cool down very slowly. Under those circumstances, it might happen that all of the sugar would remain in solution even at a temperature of 25°C. But at that temperature, the solubility of sugar is normally a little over 100 grams per 100 grams of water. Therefore, the cooled solution would be supersaturated. Supersaturated solutions are normally very unstable. The slightest movement in the solution, such as simply shaking it, can cause the excess solute to settle out of the solution.

Sonar

Sonar, an acronym for *so*und *n*avigation *a*nd *r*anging, is a system that uses sound waves to detect and locate objects underwater.

The idea of using sound to determine the depth of a lake or ocean was first proposed in the early nineteenth century. Interest in this tech-

Words to Know

Active sonar: Mode of echo location by sending a signal and detecting the returning echo.

Passive sonar: Sensitive listening-only mode to detect the presence of objects making noise.

Ultrasound: Acoustic vibrations with frequencies higher than the human threshold of hearing.

nique, called underwater ranging, was renewed in 1912 when the luxury sailing vessel *Titanic* collided with an iceberg and sank. Two years later, during World War I (1914–18), a single German submarine sank three British cruisers carrying more than 1,200 men. In response, the British government funded a massive effort to create an underwater detection system.

The entire operation was conducted in complete secrecy, but the first working model was not ready until after the war ended. The project operated under the code name "asdic" (which stood for Allied Submarine Detection Investigating Committee). The device kept that name until the late 1950s, when the American term "sonar" was adopted.

How it works

The principle behind sonar is simple: a pulse of ultrasonic waves is sent into the water where it bounces off a target and comes back to the source (ultrasonic waves are pitched too high for humans to detect). The distance and location can be calculated by measuring the time it takes for the sound to return. By knowing the speed of sound in water, the distance is computed by multiplying the speed by one-half of the time traveled (for a one-way trip). This is active sonar ranging (echolocation).

Most moving objects underwater make some kind of noise. Marine life, cavitation (small collapsing air pockets caused by propellers), hull popping of submarines changing depth, and engine vibration are all forms of underwater noise. In passive sonar ranging, no pulse signal is sent. Instead, the searcher listens for the characteristic sound of another boat or submarine. By doing so, the searcher can identify the target without revealing his own location. This method is most often used during wartime.

However, since a submarine is usually completely submerged, it must use active sonar at times, generally to navigate past obstacles. In doing so, the submarine risks alerting others of its presence. In such cases, the use of sonar has become a sophisticated military tactical exercise.

Sonar devices have become standard equipment for most commercial and many recreational ships. Fishing boats use active sonar to locate schools of fish. Other applications of sonar include searching for shipwrecks, probing harbors where visibility is poor, mapping the ocean floor, and helping submerged vessels navigate under the Arctic Ocean ice sheets.

[*See also* **Ultrasonics**]

South America

South America, the fourth largest continent on Earth, encompasses an area of 6,880,706 square miles (17,821,028 square kilometers). This is almost 12 percent of the surface area of Earth. At its widest point, the continent extends about 3,200 miles (5,150 kilometers). South America is divided into 12 independent countries: Argentina, Bolivia, Brazil, Chile, Colombia, Ecuador, Guyana, Paraguay, Peru, Suriname, Uruguay, and Venezuela. French Guiana, an overseas department (territory) of France, also occupies the continent.

The continent of South America can be divided into three main regions with distinct environmental and geological qualities. These are the eastern highlands and plateaus, the large Amazon River and its basin in the central part of the continent, and the great Andes mountain range of the western coast.

The highlands and plateaus

The eastern highlands and plateaus are the oldest geological region of South America. They are believed to have bordered on the African continent at one time, before the motion of the plates that make up Earth's crust began separating the continents about 140 million years ago. The eastern highlands and plateaus can be divided into three main sections.

The Guiana Highlands are in the northeast, in south Venezuela and northeastern Brazil. They are about 1,200 miles (1,930 kilometers) long and from 200 to 600 miles (320 to 965 kilometers) wide. Their highest peak, Mount Roraima, reaches a height of 9,220 feet (2,810 meters). This is a moist region with many rivers and waterfalls. It is in this range, in

Opposite Page: South America. (Reproduced by permission of The Gale Group.)

Caribbean Sea

North
Atlantic
Ocean

Isthmus
of
Panama

Angel Falls

Orinoco River

VENEZUELA

GUYANA

SURINAME

FRENCH GUIANA (FRANCE)

COLOMBIA

ECUADOR

Amazon River

Galapagos
Islands

PERU

BRAZIL

Andes Mountains

Brazilian Highlands

South
Pacific
Ocean

BOLIVIA

Lake Titicaca

Atacama
desert

CHILE

PARAGUAY

Mt. Aconcagua

Valparaiso

Santiago

URUGUAY

ARGENTINA

Pampas

Concepcion

South
Atlantic
Ocean

FALKLAND
ISLANDS (U.K.)

Straits of
Magellan

Tierra del Fuego

SOUTH
GEORGIA
ISLAND (U.K.)

Venezuela, that the highest waterfall in the world is found. Called Angel Falls, it cascades freely for 3,212 feet (980 meters).

The great Plateau of Brazil covers more than one-half of the area of Brazil, and ranges in altitude between 1,000 and 5,000 feet (305 and 1524 meters). The highest mountain range of this highland region is called Serra da Mantiqueira, and its highest peak, Pico das Agulhas Negras, is 9,141 feet (2,786 meters) above sea level.

The Plateau of Patagonia is in the south, in Argentina. The dominant mountain range of this highland area is Sierras de Cordoba. Its highest peak, Champaqui, reaches an altitude of 9,459 feet (2,883 meters).

The Amazon basin

The Amazon basin (the area drained by the Amazon River) is the largest river basin in the world. It covers an area of about 2,500,000 square miles (6,475,000 square kilometers), or almost 35 percent of the land area of South America. The volume of water that flows from the basin into the Atlantic is about 11 percent of all the water drained from the continents of Earth. The greatest flow occurs in July, and the lowest in November.

The Amazon basin was once an enormous bay, before the Andes Mountains were pushed up along the coast by the movement of the crust-forming plates. As the mountain range grew, it held back the ocean and eventually the bay became an inland sea. This sea was finally filled by the erosion of the higher land surrounding it, and finally a huge plain, crisscrossed by countless waterways, was created. Most of this region is still at sea level and is covered by lush jungle and extensive wetlands. This jungle region contains the largest rain forest in the world, which is home to an uncounted number of plant and animal species found nowhere else in the world.

While there are many rivers flowing through the basin, the most important and well-known of these is the Amazon River. It runs for about 3,900 miles (6,275 kilometers), from the Andes Mountains in northern Peru to the Atlantic Ocean near Belem, Brazil. When it enters the ocean, the Amazon discharges about 7,000,000 cubic feet (198,240 cubic meters) of water per second. The width of the Amazon ranges from about 1 to 8 miles (1.6 to 13 kilometers). Although the Amazon is usually only about 20 to 40 feet (6 to 12 meters) deep, there are narrow channels where it can reach a depth of 300 feet (91 meters). Almost every year, the Amazon floods, filling a flood plain up to 30 miles (48 kilometers) wide. The fresh layer of river silt deposited by the flood makes the surrounding region extremely fertile.

The Andes

The Andes Mountains constitute South America's great mountain range. They extend more than 5,000 miles (8,045 kilometers) up the western coast of the continent, passing through seven countries—Argentina, Chile, Bolivia, Peru, Ecuador, Colombia, and Venezuela. The highest peak of the Andes, called Mount Aconcagua, is on the western side of central Argentina, and is 22,835 feet (6,960 meters) high. Lake Titicaca, the world's highest large freshwater lake, is located in the Andes on the border between Peru and Bolivia at a height of 12,500 feet (3,800 meters) above sea level.

Iguazu Falls on Argentina's border with Paraguay and Brazil. *(Reproduced by permission of Susan D. Rock.)*

The Andes were formed by the motion of crustal plates. Millions of years ago, the South American plate (on which the continent sits) broke away from the African plate. When the western edge of the South American plate met the eastern edge of the Nazca plate under the Pacific Ocean, the Nazca plate subducted or slid under the South American plate. (Since continental plates are less dense than oceanic plates, they ride over them.) This motion caused the western edge of the South American plate to buckle, fold, and be thrust upwards, forming the Andes Mountains. As the Nazca plate continues to sink under the surface, its leading edge is melted by the extreme temperatures and pressures inside Earth. Molten rock then rises to the surface, lifting and deforming it. To this day, the Andes are still rising.

This geological instability makes earthquakes common all along the western region of the continent. The Andes are dotted with volcanoes. Some of the highest peaks in the mountain range, which rise above 20,000 feet (6,100 meters), are volcanic in origin. The Andes in Chile contain the greatest concentration of volcanoes on the continent: over 2,000 active and dormant volcanoes. The area is plagued by earthquakes.

The climate in the Andes varies greatly, depending on both altitude and latitude, from hot regions to Alpine meadow regions to glacier regions. The snowline is highest in southern Peru and northern Chili, where it seldom descends below 19,000 feet (5,800 meters). In the far south of the continent, in the region known as Tierra del Fuego, the snowline reaches as low as 2,000 feet (600 meters) above sea level.

The Andes are a rich source of mineral deposits, particularly copper, silver, tin, iron, and gold. The Andes in Colombia yield rich deposits of coal, while in Venezuela they contain petroleum. The largest deposits of emeralds in the world, outside of Russia, are found in the Colombian Andes. The Andes are also a source of tungsten, antimony, nickel, chromium, cobalt, and sulfur.

[*See also* **Plate tectonics**]

Space

The term space has two general meanings. First, it refers to the three-dimensional extension in which all things exist and move. We sometimes speak about outer space as everything that exists outside our own solar system. But the term space in astronomy and in everyday conversation can also refer to everything that makes up the universe, including our own solar system and Earth.

Mathematicians also speak about space in an abstract sense and try to determine properties that can be attributed to it. Although they most commonly refer to three-dimensional space, no mathematical reason exists not to study two-dimensional, one-dimensional, four-dimensional, or even n-dimensional (an unlimited number of dimensions) space.

Space-time continuum

One of the most important scientific discoveries of the twentieth century had to do with the nature of space. Traditionally, both scientists and nonscientists thought of space and time as being two different and generally unrelated phenomena. A person might describe where he or she is in terms of three-dimensional space: at the corner of Lithia Way and East Main Street in Ashland, for example. Or he or she might say what time it is: 4:00 P.M. on April 14.

What the great German-born American physicist Albert Einstein (1879–1955) showed was that space and time are really part of the same way of describing the universe. Instead of talking about space or time, one needed to talk about one's place on the space-time continuum. That is, we move about in four dimensions, the three physical dimensions with which we are familiar and a fourth dimension—the dimension of time.

Einstein's conception of space-time dramatically altered the way scientists thought about many aspects of the physical world. For example, it suggested a new way of defining gravity. Instead of being a force between two objects, Einstein said, gravity must be thought of in terms of irregularities in the space-time continuum of the universe. As objects pass through these irregularities, they exhibit behaviors that correspond almost exactly to the effects that we once knew as gravitational attraction.

[See also **Big bang theory; Cosmology; Relativity; Time**]

Spacecraft, manned

Since 1961, hundreds of men and women from more than a dozen countries have traveled in space. Until the 1980s, however, most of those people came from the United States and the former Soviet Union. The Soviets were the first to launch an unmanned satellite, *Sputnik 1,* in 1957. This event marked the beginning of the space race between the United States and the Soviet Union, a campaign for superiority in space exploration.

The first living being to travel in space was a dog named Laika. She was sent into space aboard the Soviets' *Sputnik 2* in 1957. Laika survived the launch and the first leg of the journey. A week after launch, however, the air supply ran out and Laika suffocated. When the spacecraft reentered Earth's atmosphere in April 1958, it burned up (it had no heat shields) and Laika's body was incinerated.

Then on April 12, 1961, Soviet cosmonaut (astronaut) Yury Gagarin rode aboard the *Vostok 1,* becoming the first human in space. In 108 minutes, he made a single orbit around Earth before reentering its atmosphere. At about two miles (more than three kilometers) above the ground, he parachuted to safety. Only recently did scientists from outside Russia learn that this seemingly flawless mission almost ended in disaster. During its final descent, the spacecraft had spun wildly out of control.

American-crewed space program

The Mercury program was the first phase of America's effort to put a human on the Moon by the end of the 1960s. On May 5, 1961, the first

Sputnik I was the first unmanned satellite to be launched, by the Soviet Union in 1957. *(Reproduced by permission of Corbis-Bettmann.)*

piloted Mercury flight, *Freedom 7,* was launched. It took astronaut Alan Shepard on a 15-minute suborbital flight (only a partial—not complete—orbit of Earth) that went 116 miles (187 kilometers) up and 303 miles (488 kilometers) across the Atlantic Ocean at speeds up to 5,146 miles (8,280 kilometers) per hour. The capsule than parachuted safely into the Atlantic Ocean with Shepard inside.

Two months later, another U.S. suborbital flight was launched, this one carrying Virgil "Gus" Grissom. Grissom's flight was similar to Shepard's, except at splashdown his capsule took in water and sank. Grissom was unharmed, but his capsule, the *Liberty Bell 7,* was not recovered.

On February 20, 1962, just over nine months after Gagarin's flight, astronaut John Glenn became the first American to orbit Earth. His spacecraft, *Friendship 7,* completed three orbits in less than five hours.

Lunar program. The Apollo program was created for the purpose of landing American astronauts on the Moon. Engineers designed a craft consisting of three parts: a command module, in which the astronauts would travel; a service module, which contained supplies and equipment; and a lunar module, which would detach to land on the Moon.

The Apollo program was not without mishap. During a ground test in 1967, a fire engulfed the cabin of the *Apollo 1* spacecraft, killing Gus Grissom, Ed White, and Roger Chaffee. This tragedy prompted a two-year delay in the launch of the first Apollo spacecraft. During this time, more than 1,500 modifications were made to the command module.

In December 1968, *Apollo 8* became the first manned spacecraft to orbit both Earth and the Moon. On July 16, 1969, *Apollo 11* was launched with astronauts Neil Armstrong, Edwin "Buzz" Aldrin, and Michael Collins on board. Four days later Armstrong and Aldrin landed on the Moon. When Armstrong set foot on lunar soil, he stated, "That's one small step for man, one giant leap for mankind." The *Apollo 11* flight to the Moon is considered by many to be the greatest technological achievement of the modern world. Over the next three years, five more Apollo missions landed twelve more Americans on the Moon.

Soviet-crewed space program

Although the United States won the race to the Moon, the Soviet Union achieved other space race "firsts" during the 1960s. The Soviets launched the first three-person spacecraft, *Voskhod* ("Sunrise"), in October 1964. In March 1965, Soviet cosmonaut Alexei Leonov took the first space walk, spending ten minutes outside the *Voskhod* capsule connected to the craft only by telephone and telemetry cables (wires used to gather data).

The Soviet Union then began work on Soyuz ("Union"). The program proved to be a disaster. In April 1967, *Soyuz 1* crashed to Earth with cosmonaut Vladimir Komarov on board. The tragedy halted the Soviet space program for 18 months. By the time they reentered the space flight quest, the Soviets had turned their attention to establishing the first orbiting space station, *Salyut* ("Salute").

The liftoff of *Apollo 11* from pad 39A at Kennedy Space Center on July 16, 1969, at 9:32 A.M. Crewmen Neil A. Armstrong, Michael Collins, and Edwin E. Aldrin Jr. were the first to land on the Moon. *(Reproduced by permission of National Aeronautics and Space Administration.)*

Space stations

On April 19, 1971, the Soviets launched *Salyut 1,* which was designed for both civilian and military purposes. The station was powered by two solar panels and divided into several different modules, three of which were pressurized for human life support. The three-person crew of *Soyuz 11* successfully entered *Salyut 1* on June 7, 1971. The cosmonauts' three-week stay set a new record for human endurance in space. But during their reentry into Earth's atmosphere, a cabin seal released prematurely and the spacecraft lost air pressure. The three crew members had not been issued pressure suits and suffocated instantly. As a result of this disaster, the Soviets could not refuel the station. They were forced to allow it to fall out of its orbit and burn up in reentry. Despite this major setback, the Soviets were eventually able to launch other *Salyut* stations as the decade progressed.

The only comparable U.S. space station has been *Skylab.* Launched on May 14, 1973, this two-story craft was 118 feet (36 meters) long and 21 feet (6.4 meters) in diameter and weighed nearly 100 tons (110 metric tons). Although *Skylab* encountered problems immediately after launch, a crew was able to repair the damage. In its six years of operation, *Skylab* housed three different crews for a total of 171 days. Studies on board the space station greatly increased our knowledge of the Sun and its effect on Earth's environment. In 1979, *Skylab* fell back to Earth.

A more advanced Soviet space station, *Mir* (which means both "Peace" and "World"), was launched in February 1986. Able to accommodate up to six crew members at a time, *Mir* was designed to afford greater comfort and privacy to its inhabitants so they would be able to remain on board for longer periods. Although plagued with technical problems in 1997, *Mir* continued to host Russian cosmonauts and international space travelers (a total of 104 people from 12 countries) who conducted some 23,000 experiments, including research into how humans, animals, and plants function in space. During its lengthy time in orbit, *Mir* attained a number of accomplishments: longest time in orbit for a space station (15 years), longest time in space for a human (437.7 days), and heaviest artificial object ever to orbit Earth. With a lone cosmonaut on board at the time, it even survived the collapse of the Soviet Union in 1991. During *Mir*'s lifetime, the Soviet Union and then Russia spent the equivalent of $4.2 billion to build and maintain the station. By 2001, however, the 135-ton (122-metric ton) craft had become too old to maintain properly, and Russia decided to let it fall back to Earth. On March 23, 2001, after having completed 86,330 orbits around the planet, *Mir* reentered the atmosphere and broke apart. Pieces of the station that did not burn up in the atmosphere splashed harmlessly into stormy waters 1,800 miles (2,896 kilometers) east of New Zealand.

The valuable knowledge scientists gained from *Mir* will be applied to the International Space Station (ISS), a permanent Earth-orbiting laboratory that will allow humans to perform long-term research in outer space. It draws upon the scientific and technological resources of sixteen nations. Construction of the ISS began in November 1998 with the launch of the Zarya control module from Russia. When completed in 2006, the ISS will measure about 360 feet (110 meters) in length, 290 feet (88 meters) in width, and 143 feet (44 meters) in height. It will have a mass of nearly 1 million pounds (454,000 kilograms) and will have a pressurized

The space shuttle *Atlantis* on its maiden voyage. *(Reproduced by permission of National Aeronautics and Space Administration.)*

living and working space of 46,000 cubic feet (1,300 cubic meters), enough for up to seven astronauts and scientists.

Space shuttles

The U.S. space shuttle is a winged space plane designed to transport humans into space and back. It is the first and only reusable space vehicle. This 184-foot-long (56-meter-long) vessel acts like a spacecraft, but looks like an airplane. In 1981, the first space shuttle to be launched was *Columbia. Challenger, Discovery,* and *Atlantis* rounded out the initial shuttle fleet, which flew 24 consecutive missions.

The shuttle program ran smoothly until the *Challenger* tragedy of January 28, 1986. That shuttle exploded 73 seconds after launch, due to a faulty seal in its solid rocket booster. All seven crew members died as a result. The fleet of shuttles was grounded for 32 months while more than 400 changes in the shuttle's construction were made.

The National Aeronautics and Space Administration (NASA) resumed shuttle flights in 1988, having replaced *Challenger* with *Endeavor.* Missions of the space shuttles have included the insertion into orbit of the *Galileo* space probe in 1989 and the Hubble Space Telescope (HST) in 1990. A variety of communications, weather, military, and scientific satellites have also been placed into orbit by crew members aboard space shuttles. The shuttles can be configured to carry many different types of equipment, spacecraft, and scientific experiments. In addition to transporting people, materials, equipment, and spacecraft to orbit, the shuttles allow astronauts to service and repair satellites and observatories in space. In fact, shuttles flew servicing missions to the HST in 1993, 1997, and 1999.

At the beginning of the twenty-first century, the mission of many shuttle flights was the continuing construction of the ISS. In December 1998, the crew aboard *Endeavor* initiated the first assembly sequence of the ISS; they also became the first crew to enter the space station. In October 2000, when *Discovery* was launched on a mission to continue construction of the ISS, the event marked the one-hundredth flight of a U.S. space shuttle.

[*See also* **Space station, international**]

Space probe

A space probe is any unmanned spacecraft designed to carry out physical studies of the Moon, other planets, or outer space. Space probes take pictures, measure atmospheric conditions, and collect soil samples then bring or report the data back to Earth.

More than 30 space probes have been launched since the former Soviet Union first fired *Luna 1* toward the Moon in 1959. Probes have now visited every planet in the solar system except for Pluto. Two have even left the solar system and headed into the interstellar medium.

Moon probes

The earliest probes traveled to the Moon. The Soviets launched a series of Luna probes that took the first pictures of the far side of the Moon. In 1966, *Luna 9* made the first successful landing on the Moon and sent back television footage from the Moon's surface.

The National Aeronautics and Space Administration (NASA) landed *Surveyor* on the Moon four months after *Luna 9*. The *Surveyor* had more sophisticated landing capability and sent back more than 11,000 pictures.

Planetary probes

In the meantime, NASA launched the first series of planetary probes, called Mariner. *Mariner 2* first reached Venus in 1962. Later Mariner spacecraft flew by Mars in 1964 and 1969, providing detailed images of that planet. In 1971, *Mariner 9* became the first spacecraft to orbit Mars. During its year in orbit, *Mariner 9* transmitted footage of an intense Martian dust storm as well as images of 90 percent of the planet's surface and the two Martian moons.

The Soviets also put probes in orbit around Mars in 1971. *Mars 2* and *Mars 3* carried landing vehicles that successfully dropped to the planet's surface, but in each case radio contact was lost after about 20 seconds.

In 1976, the U.S. probes *Viking 1* and *Viking 2* had more direct encounters with Mars. *Viking 1* made the first successful soft landing on Mars on July 20, 1976. Soon after, *Viking 2* landed on the opposite side of the planet. The Viking probes reported on the Martian weather and photographed almost the entire surface of the planet. Twenty years after the Voyager probes were released, NASA launched the *Mars Global Surveyor* and the *Mars Pathfinder* to revisit Mars. The *Mars Global Surveyor* completed its mapping mission of Mars in early 2001 after having sent back tens of thousands of images of the planet. Its main mission accomplished, NASA engineers hope to use *Surveyor* to relay commands to twin rovers slated to land on the planet in early 2004. The *Mars Pathfinder* landed on the planet's surface on July 4, 1997, and released the Sojourner rover, which sent back to Earth images and analyses of the Martian terrain, including chemical analyses of rocks and the soil.

Not all probe sent to Mars were as productive as the *Mars Global Surveyor* and the *Mars Pathfinder.* In 1999, NASA lost two probes, the *Mars Climate Orbiter* and the *Mars Polar Lander.* As its name implies the *Mars Climate Orbiter* was to have explored the Martian atmosphere, while the *Mars Polar Lander* was to have explored the planet's landscape in search of water. Neither was able to land successfully due to an error in converting English and metric measurements (for the *Mars Climate Orbiter*) and a software glitch (for the *Mars Polar Lander*).

From 1970 to 1983, the Soviets concentrated mostly on exploring Venus. They sent out a series of Venera and Vega probes that landed on Venus, analyzed its oil, took detailed photographs, studied the atmosphere, and mapped the planet using radar.

Mercury was visited by a probe in 1974 when *Mariner 10* came within 470 miles (756 kilometers) of the planet and photographed about 40 percent of its surface. The probe then went into orbit around the Sun and flew past Mercury twice more in the next year before running out of fuel.

The space probe *Mariner 10,* launched November 3, 1973, was first to travel to Mercury. *(Reproduced by permission of National Aeronautics and Space Administration.)*

Space probes to the outer planets

NASA sent Pioneer probes to explore the outer planets. *Pioneer 10* reached Jupiter in 1973 and took the first close-up photos of the giant planet. It then kept traveling, crossing the orbit of Pluto and leaving the solar system in 1983. *Pioneer 11* traveled to Saturn, where it collected valuable information about the planet's rings.

NASA next introduced the *Voyager 1* and *2* probes, more sophisticated versions of the Pioneers. Launched in 1977, they flew by Jupiter two years later and took pictures of the planet's swirling colors, volcanic moons, and its previously undiscovered ring.

The Voyager space probes then headed for Saturn. In 1980 and 1981, they sent back detailed photos of Saturn's spectacular rings and its vast collection of moons. *Voyager 2* then traveled to Neptune, which it reached in 1989, while *Voyager 1* continued on a path to the edge of the solar system and beyond.

After many delays, the U.S probe *Galileo* was launched from the space shuttle *Atlantis* in 1989. It reached Jupiter in December 1995, and dropped a barbecue-grill-sized mini-probe down to the planet's surface. That mini-probe spent 58 minutes taking extremely detailed pictures of the gaseous planet before being incinerated near the surface. As of the

The interplanetary probe *Voyager* explored the regions of space around Jupiter, Saturn, and Uranus. *(Reproduced by permission of National Aeronautics and Space Administration.)*

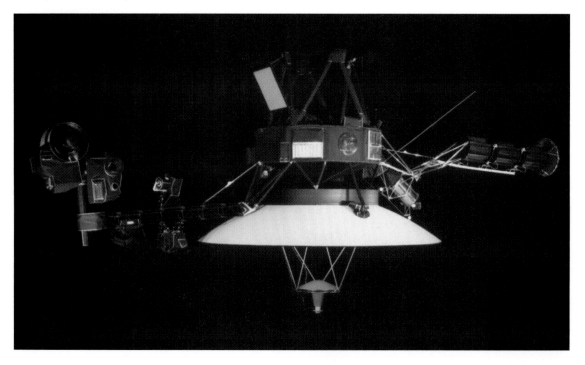

beginning of 2001, *Galileo* was still sending valuable scientific information about Jupiter and its moons back to Earth.

In February 1996, NASA launched NEAR (Near Earth Asteroid Rendezvous) Shoemaker, an unmanned spacecraft that was to become the first to orbit an asteroid. In April 2000, it began a circular orbit around the asteroid Eros. During its one-year mission around Eros, the spacecraft took measurements to determine the mass, density, chemical composition, and other geological characteristics of the asteroid. It also beamed some 160,000 images of Eros back to Earth. In February 2001, NEAR Shoemaker used the last of its fuel in a successful attempt to land on the surface of the asteroid. Once on the surface, it continued to collect invaluable data about the oddly shaped Eros before it was finally shut down by NASA.

Future space probe missions

NASA has plans underway for many more space probes. The *Cassini* orbiter, which was launched in October 1997, will study Saturn and its moon. It is scheduled to reach the planet in 2004. *Cassini* will drop a mini-probe, called *Huygens,* onto the surface of Titan, Saturn's largest moon, for a detailed look. *Cassini* will then go into orbit around Saturn.

With a desire to return to Mars, NASA launched the *Mars Odyssey* in April 2001. Once in orbit around the planet by the fall of that year, the spacecraft will examine the composition of the planet's surface and try to detect water and shallow buried ice. In a mission planned by the European Space Agency and the Italian space agency, NASA will launch the *Mars Express* in mid-2003. It will search for subsurface water from orbit and deliver a lander, Beagle 2, to the Martian surface. NASA will also launch two powerful rovers to Mars in 2003, each to a different region of the planet to look for water. And in 2005, NASA plans to launch the *Mars Reconnaissance Orbiter,* a powerful scientific orbiter that will map the Martian surface with an high-definition camera.

NASA had hoped to explore Pluto sometime in the twenty-first century by sending the *Pluto-Kuiper Express.* This probe was to have consisted of two spacecraft, each taking about eight years to reach the farthest planet in our solar system. Originally scheduled to launch in 2004 and arrive at Pluto in 2012, the *Pluto-Kuiper Express* was put on hold by NASA in the fall of 2000 because of high costs. It was then scraped in the spring of 2001 after President George W. Bush unveiled his 2002 budget, which provided no money for the project.

[*See also* **Jupiter; Mars; Mercury; Moon; Neptune; Pluto; Satellite; Saturn; Spacecraft, manned; Venus**]

Space station, international

The International Space Station (ISS) is a permanent Earth-orbiting laboratory that will allow humans to perform long-term research in outer space. Led by the United States, the ISS draws upon the scientific and technological resources of sixteen nations. When completed in 2006, it will be the largest and most complex international scientific project in history.

Origins

The International Space Station had its beginnings in the cold war rivalry (period of silent conflict and tension) that existed between the United States and the then Soviet Union (also called the U.S.S.R.) from the 1950s to the 1990s. Although the United States was the first to put a man on the Moon (1969), the Soviet Union came to specialize in and dominate the field of long-term human spaceflight. As early as 1971, they successfully launched the world's first orbiting space station (*Salyut 1*) and continued nearly uninterrupted through the 1990s. Where the United States has placed only one space station in orbit (*Skylab* in 1973) and sent only three crews of three astronauts to live there (none longer than eighty-four days), the Soviet Union gained valuable space station experience by regularly shuttling crews to its three generations of stations. One crew member remained in space for a 438-day tour.

Around the mid-1980s, the United States decided to compete against and try to outdistance the Soviet Union in the space station field, since it felt that a long-term manned presence in space was what its military would need in the future. The United States invited other nations (except the Soviet Union) to participate on what it called Space Station Freedom. When the it collapsed and broke apart in 1991, the former Soviet Union (now called Russia) was eventually invited to join the effort. Since the Russian Space Agency faced severe financial problems (as did all of Russia after the break-up), it accepted help from the United States and eventually agreed to join and lend its vast experience to the creation of a truly international station in space.

ISS goals

In 1993, the United States put forth a detailed long-range ISS plan that included substantial Russian participation as well as the involvement of fourteen other nations. Altogether sixteen countries—Belgium, Brazil, Canada, Denmark, France, Germany, Italy, Japan, the Netherlands, Norway, Russia, Spain, Sweden, Switzerland, the United Kingdom, and the

United States—have banded together on a non-military effort so complex and expensive that no one nation could ever consider doing it alone. The program will involve more than 100,000 people in space agencies and contracting companies around the world. It is expected to cost at least $40 billion and take nearly a decade to complete.

The ISS project has lofty goals. It is expected that having long-term, uninterrupted access to outer space will allow investigators to acquire large sets of data in weeks that would have taken years to obtain. The ISS project also plans to conduct medical and industrial experiments that it hopes will result in benefits to all humankind.

ISS systems and size

The ambitious ISS has been likened in difficulty to building a pyramid in the zero gravity or weightlessness of outer space. When completely assembled, the ISS will have a mass of nearly 1 million pounds (454,000 kilograms) and will be about 360 feet (110 meters) across by 290 feet (88

United States International Space Station (ISS) Cooperation Phase III, containing elements from the United States, Europe, Canada, and Russia. *(Reproduced by permission of National Aeronautics and Space Administration.)*

meters) long, making it much wider than the length of a football field. This large scale means that it can provide 46,000 cubic feet (1,300 cubic meters) of pressurized living and working space for a crew of seven scientists and engineers. This amount of usable space is greater than the volume of the passenger cabin and cargo hold of a huge Boeing 747-400 aircraft. This massive structure will get its power from nearly an acre of solar panels spread out on four photovoltaic (pronounced foe-toe-vole-TAY-ik) modules. These solar arrays rotate to always face the Sun and can convert sunlight into electricity that can be stored in batteries. The station will have fifty-two computers controlling its many systems.

The main components of the ISS are the Service Module, which is Russia's first contribution, and then six scientific laboratories (one American, one European Space Agency, one Japanese, and three Russian labs). The other major contributor is Canada, which is providing a 55-foot-long (16.7-meter-long) robotic arm for assembly and other maintenance tasks. The United States also has the responsibility for developing and ultimately operating all the major elements and systems aboard the station. More than forty space flights over five years will be required to deliver these and many other space station components to the orbiting altitude of 250 miles (402 kilometers) above Earth.

Assembly in space

The Russians placed the first major piece of the puzzle—the control module named Zarya—in orbit during November 1998. Following the launch of the American module named Unity during December of that year (which would serve as the connecting passageway between sections), the Russians launched their service module named Zvezda in July 2000. This not only provided life support systems to other elements but also served as early living quarters for the first crew. After more flights to deliver supplies and equipment, the American laboratory module named Destiny was docked with the station during February 2001. This state-of-the-art facility will be the centerpiece of the station. The aluminum lab is 28 feet (8.5 meters) long and 14 feet (4.3 meters) wide and will allow astronauts to work in a year-round shirtsleeve environment. Following the addition of a pressurized laboratory built by the European Space Agency, the robotic arm built by Canada, and a Japanese Experiment Module, the station will have many of its most important working components assembled.

Uses of space research

Since the main goal of the ISS is to conduct long-term scientific research in space, the crews naturally have a great deal of research to perform. Some examples of the type of research conducted are protein crystal studies. It is believed that since zero gravity allows more pure protein crystals to be grown in space than on Earth, analysis of these crystals may lead to the development of new drugs and a better understanding of the fundamental building blocks of life. Growing living cells in zero gravity is also a benefit since they are not distorted by gravity. Astronauts can therefore grow tissue cultures aboard the station that can be used to test new treatments for cancer without risking harm to patients.

Astronauts will also be testing themselves and learning more about the effects of long-term exposure to reduced gravity on humans. Studying how muscles weaken and what changes occur in the heart, arteries, veins, and bones may not only lead to a better understanding of the body's systems, but might help us plan for future long-term human exploration of the solar system.

Flames, fluids, and metals all act differently in zero gravity, and astronauts will be conducting research in what is called Materials Science to try to create better alloys. The nature of space itself will be studied by examining what happens to the exterior of a spacecraft over time. Also of great interest are the physics of forces that are difficult to study when they are subject to the gravity of Earth. New products will regularly be sought after, and there is hope that space may have real commercial potential that might lead to the creation of industry in space.

Lastly, Earth itself will be watched and examined. Studying its forests, oceans, and mountains from space may lead us to better understand the large-scale, long-term changes that take place in our environment. We can also study how badly we are harming our planet with air and water pollution and by the cutting and burning of forests. The ISS will have four large windows designed just for looking at Earth.

The future in space

The assembly in space of such a huge station has begun a new era of hands-on work in space. More spacewalks than ever before will have to be conducted (about 850 hours will be required before the astronauts are finished). Already, Earth orbit has literally become a day-to-day construction site. Once completed, the ISS will be permanently crewed, and the crews will rotate during crew-exchange flights. The outgoing crew will "handover" the station to the incoming crew.

During the first few years, emergencies that require crew evacuation will be handled by always having a Russian Soyuz return capsule onboard. Eventually this will be replaced by an X-38 Crew Return Vehicle that will look more like an airplane (as the space shuttle does) and will function as an all-purpose space pickup truck. Finally, despite the best of plans, there is always the possibility that the space station may not be fully completed due to any number of political, engineering, or financial reasons. Designers therefore have taken this into account and have planned the project so that it can still be fully used despite only limited completion.

[*See also* **Spacecraft, manned**]

Spectroscopy

Spectroscopy is a science concerned with the analysis of the composition of matter based on the kind of radiation emitted by that matter. For example, suppose that a piece of iron is heated until it begins to glow. The light given off by the iron is a characteristic property of iron. That is, the light is different from light produced by any other metal such as copper, tin, lead, uranium, or aluminum.

The spectroscope

In heated samples of iron, copper, tin, and other metals, the light produced does not look very different from one metal to the next. The differences that do exist in these cases can be detected only by using a special instrument known as a spectroscope. The structure of one type of spectroscope is shown in Figure 1.

Light produced from some source (such as a heated metal) is first passed through a narrow slit. The slit causes the light to spread out, form-

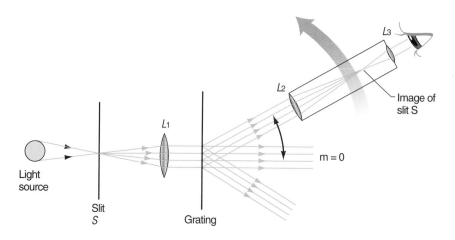

Figure 1. (Reproduced by permission of The Gale Group.)

Words to Know

Absorption spectrum: The spectrum formed when light passes through a cool gas.

Diffraction grating: A device consisting of a surface into which are etched very fine, closely spaced grooves that cause different wavelengths of light to reflect or refract (bend) by different amounts.

Emission spectrum: The colors of light emitted by a heated gas.

Spectrograph: An instrument for recording spectra.

Spectrometer: An instrument that records the wavelengths (or frequencies) and intensities of radiation emitted or absorbed by a sample.

ing a set of diverging rays. Those rays are caused to fall on a lens (L_1 in the figure), which makes them parallel to each other. The parallel rays then fall on a grating, a piece of glass or plastic into which hundreds or thousands of very narrow parallel grooves are etched.

The grating acts like a glass prism, causing the light to break apart into a whole range of colors. If the light coming from the source were pure white light, the grating would break it up into a continuous spectrum, a rainbowlike array containing every color from violet to red.

Finally, the spectrum—the spread of colored light—can be viewed through a small telescope (L_2 and L_3 in the figure). Or it can be recorded on a piece of photographic film on a device known as a spectrograph for later study. In many cases, the actual wavelengths present in a spectrum— and the intensity of each one—can be recorded by means of an instrument known as a spectrometer.

Emission and absorption spectra

A continuous spectrum is produced only when a great many different elements and compounds are heated together all at the same time. When a single element or a single compound is heated all by itself, a different kind of spectrum—a line spectrum—is produced. A line spectrum consists of a number of lines located at various specific angles in the range from blue to red. For example, hydrogen produces two lines in the blue region of the spectrum, another line in the green region, and a fourth line in the red region of the spectrum. In contrast, sodium produces only two lines, both in the yellow region of the spectrum.

These lines are called emission spectra because they are produced when an element gives off light. Every element has a distinctive emission spectrum, like those described for hydrogen and sodium. If a scientist views the emission spectrum produced by some unknown material, he or she can refer to a chart of emission spectra of the elements. The spectrum from the unknown material can be compared to those in the chart, allowing the scientist to identify the unknown.

One can also study absorption spectra. Imagine an experiment in which a white light is shined through a gas. The light passing through the gas is then studied by means of a spectrometer. In this case, the light that is recorded consists of all of the white light that came from the original source less any light absorbed by the gas through which it passed.

Again, the spectrum observed in this experiment is a line spectrum. In this case, however, the lines observed are those that are *not* absorbed by the gas between the light source and the observer.

Types of spectroscopy

As described above, all elements have distinctive line spectra. It happens that all compounds have distinctive spectra as well. If one were to heat a sample of iron oxide instead of pure iron metal, the same experiment as the one described above could be conducted. In this case, the line spectrum produced would be that of the compound iron metal rather than the element iron.

Light spectroscopy, the technique described so far, has its limitations. When some elements and compounds are heated, they produce spectra that lie outside the visible spectrum. In some cases, lines are produced in the infrared, ultraviolet, or even X-ray region of the electromagnetic spectrum. Special techniques and instruments have been developed to analyze spectra produced in all of these ranges.

[*See also* **Diffraction; Electromagnetic spectrum; Qualitative analysis**]

Spectrum

The term spectrum has two different, but closely related, meanings. In general, the term refers to a whole range of things. In everyday life, for

Words to Know

Absorption spectrum: The spectrum formed when light passes through a cool gas.

Continuous spectrum: A spectrum that consists of every possible wavelength of light or energy.

Electromagnetic spectrum: The continuous distribution of all electromagnetic radiation with wavelengths ranging from approximately 10^{-15} to 10^{6} meters, which includes gamma rays, X rays, ultraviolet, visible light, infrared, microwaves, and radio waves.

Emission spectrum: The spectrum produced when atoms are excited and give off energy.

Frequency: For a wave, the number of crests (or troughs) that pass a stationary point per second.

Line spectrum: A spectrum that consists of a few discrete lines.

Wavelength: The distance between adjacent peaks (peaks located next to each other) or troughs on a wave.

example, a person might say that he or she is interested in the whole spectrum of news stories, meaning that he or she enjoys reading and hearing about anything to do with the news.

In the field of science, one meaning for the word spectrum has to do with the whole range of electromagnetic energies that exist. This range is known as the electromagnetic spectrum. All forms of electromagnetic energy travel through space in the form of waves that have distinctive wavelengths and frequencies. The wavelength of a wave is the distance between adjacent identical parts of the wave, as between two crests or two troughs (pronounced trawfs). The frequency of a wave is the number of crests (or troughs) that pass a given point in space per second.

The electromagnetic spectrum consists of forms of energy such as gamma rays, X rays, ultraviolet radiation, infrared radiation, visible light, radio waves, microwaves, and radar. These forms of energy are similar in their mode of transmission but different from each other in their wavelength and frequency.

The term spectrum is also used in describing the whole range of visible light, ranging from red through orange, yellow, green, and blue to violet. If all colors are represented in the spectrum, it is called a continuous spectrum. A rainbow is an example of a continuous spectrum.

When any one given element is heated, it also gives off a spectrum—but one that is not continuous. Instead, it gives off a series of lines that reflect specific electron changes that occur within the atoms of that element. Some elements have very simple line spectra consisting of only a handful of lines. Other elements give off more complex line spectra with many lines.

Line spectra can take on one of two general forms: emission or absorption spectra. An emission spectrum is the line pattern formed when an element is excited and gives off energy. An absorption spectrum is formed when white light passes through a cool gas. The gas absorbs certain wavelengths of energy and allows others to pass through. The line spectrum formed by the energy that passes through the gas is known as an absorption spectrum.

[*See also* **Electromagnetic spectrum; Light; Spectroscopy**]

Speech

Speech is defined as the ability to communicate thoughts, ideas, or other information by means of sounds that have clear meaning to others.

Many animals make sounds that might seem to be a form of speech. For example, one may sound an alarm that a predator is in the area. The sound warns others of the same species that an enemy is in their territory. Or an animal may make soothing sounds to let offspring know that a parent is present. Most scientists regard these sounds as something other than true speech.

Some animals can copy human speech to a certain extent also. Many birds, for example, can repeat words that they have been taught. This form of mimicry also does not qualify as true speech.

True speech consists of two essential elements. First, an organism has to be able to develop and phrase thoughts to be expressed. Second, the organism has to have the anatomical equipment with which to utter clear words that convey those thoughts. Most scientists believe that humans are the only species capable of speech.

Speech has been a critical element in the evolution of the human species. It is a means by which a people's history can be handed down from one generation to the next. It enables one person to convey knowledge to a roomful of other people. It can be used to amuse, to rouse, to

Words to Know

Anatomical structure: A part of the body.

Aphasia: The inability to express or understand speech or the written word.

Broca's area: The part of the brain that controls the anatomical structures that make speech possible.

Epiglottis: The flap at the top of the larynx that regulates air movement and prevents food from entering the trachea.

Larynx: A tube that joins the trachea to the lower part of the mouth.

Palate: The roof of the mouth.

Trachea: The windpipe; a tube that joins the larynx to the lungs.

Vocal cords: Muscular folds of tissue located in the larynx involved in the production of sounds.

anger, to express sadness, to communicate needs that arise between two or more humans.

The anatomy of speech

Spoken words are produced when air expelled from the lungs passes through a series of structures within the chest and throat and passes out through the mouth. The structures involved in that process are as follows: air that leaves the lungs travels up the trachea (windpipe) into the larynx. (The larynx is a longish tube that joins the trachea to the lower part of the mouth.) Two sections of the larynx consist of two thick, muscular folds of tissue known as the vocal cords. When a person is simply breathing, the vocal cords are relaxed. Air passes through them easily without producing a sound.

When a person wishes to say a word, muscles in the vocal cords tighten up. Air that passes through the tightened vocal cords begins to vibrate, producing a sound. The nature of that sound depends on factors such as how much air is pushed through the vocal cords and how tightly the vocal cords are stretched.

The moving air—now a form of sound—passes upward and out of the larynx. A flap at the top of the larynx, the epiglottis, opens and closes to allow air to enter and leave the larynx. The epiglottis is closed when a person is eating—preventing food from passing into the larynx and trachea—but is open when a person breathes or speaks.

Once a sound leaves the vocal cords, it is altered by other structures in the mouth, such as the tongue and lips. A person can form these structures into various shapes to make different sounds. Saying the letters "d," "m," and "p" exemplifies how your lips and tongues are involved in this process.

Other parts of the mouth also contribute to the sound that is finally produced. These parts include the soft palate (roof) at the back of the mouth, the hard or bony palate in the front, and the teeth. The nose also provides an alternate means of issuing sound and is part of the production of speech. Movement of the entire lower jaw can alter the size of the mouth cavern and influence the tone and volume of the speech.

The tongue is the most agile body part in forming sounds. It is a powerful muscle that can take many shapes—flat, convex, curled—and can move front and back to contact the palate, teeth, or gums. The front of the tongue may move upward to contact the hard palate while the back of the tongue is depressed. Essentially these movements open or obstruct the passage of air through the mouth. During speech, the tongue moves rapidly and changes shapes constantly to form partial or complete closure of the vocal tract necessary to manufacture words.

The brain

Other animals have anatomical structures similar to those described above. Yet, they do not speak. The reason that they lack speech is that they lack the brain development needed to form ideas that can be expressed in words.

In humans, the part of the brain that controls the anatomical structures that make speech possible is known as Broca's area. It is located in the left hemisphere (half) of the brain for right-handed and most left-handed people. Nerves from Broca's area lead to the neck and face and control movements of the tongue, lips, and jaws.

The portion of the brain in which language is recognized is situated in the right hemisphere. This separation leads to an interesting phenomenon: a person who loses the capacity for speech still may be able to understand what is spoken to him or her and vice versa. The loss of the power of speech or the ability to understand speech or the written word is called aphasia.

Three speech disorders result from damage to the speech center, dysarthria, dysphonia, and aphasia. Dysarthria is an inability to speak clearly because of weakness in the muscles that form words. Dysphonia is a hoarseness of the voice that can be caused by a brain tumor or any number of other factors. And aphasia can be either the inability to express thoughts in speech or writing or the inability to read or to understand speech.

[*See also* **Brain**]

Sponges

Sponges are primitive multicellular animals that live in water. All adult sponges are sessile (fixed to one spot), most being attached to hard surfaces such as rocks, corals, or shells. More than 4,500 living species are known. Although some species occur in freshwater, the vast majority are marine, living mainly in shallow tropical waters. Sponges have an amazing power of regeneration: they are capable of growing into a new individual from even the tiniest fragment of the original body.

Sponges vary widely in shape and composition. Some are tall, extending far into the water. Others are low and spread out over a surface. Some have branchlike forms while others appear like intricately formed latticework. Many others are goblet shaped. Despite their differing appearances, all sponges have a definite skeleton that provides a framework that supports the animal. In some species, this skeleton is made up of a complex arrangement of spicules, which are spiny strengthening rods with a crystalline appearance. The soft spongy material that makes up the skeleton of many species of sponges is known as spongin. The fibrous meshwork of this material makes it ideal for holding water.

Most sponges consist of an outer wall dotted with many pores or openings of different sizes. These allow the free passage of water into the central part of the body, the atrium or spongocoel (pronounced SPUN-joe-seel). Although water enters the body through a large number of openings, it always leaves through a single opening, the osculum, at the top of the body.

Sponges rely on large volumes of water passing through their bodies every day, since all sponges feed by filtering tiny plankton from the water. This same water also provides the animals with a continuous supply of oxygen and removes all body wastes as it leaves the sponge.

Sponges reproduce either sexually or asexually. In sexual reproduction, a male sponge releases a large amount of sperm cells in a dense cloud. As these cells are transported by the water currents, some enter female sponges of the same species. They are then transported to special egg chambers where fertilization may take place. Once developed, a free-swimming larva emerges and is carried away by the currents until it finds a suitable surface on which to attach.

In asexual reproduction, new offspring are produced through the process known as branching or budding off. A parent sponge produces a large number of tiny cells called gemmules, each of which is capable of developing into a new sponge. A simple sponge, for example, sprouts horizontal branches that spread out over nearby rocks and give rise to a large colony of upright, vase-shaped sponges.

Humans have used sponges for bathing, drinking, and scrubbing since ancient times. Most sponges of this sort originate in the Mediterranean and Caribbean Seas and off the coast of Florida. Although synthetic (human-made) sponges are now commonly sold, sponge fishing is still a major industry in many countries.

A vase sponge with a small blenny swimming in it and a brittle star living in it. (Reproduced by permission of Photo Researchers, Inc.)

Star

A star is a hot, roughly spherical ball of gas that shines as a result of nuclear fusion reactions in its core. Stars are one of the fundamental objects in the universe. Stars—and indeed the entire universe—are made mostly of hydrogen, the simplest and lightest element. By contrast, our bodies are composed of many complex elements, such as carbon, nitrogen, calcium, and iron. These elements are created in the cores of stars, and the final act in the lives of many stars is a massive explosion that distributes the elements it has created into the galaxy. Eventually these elements may form another star, or a planet, or life on that planet.

Star birth

Stars are born in the interstellar medium, the region of space between stars. Drifting through this region are vast, dark clouds of gas and dust. Certain celestial events, like the nearby explosion of a massive star at the end of its life (supernova), cause these clouds to begin to contract. After a supernova, a shock wave sweeps through the interstellar medium. When it slams into the cloud, the gas and dust is violently compressed by the shock. As the particles are squeezed together, their mutual gravitational attraction grows and a blob of gas forms, giving off energy.

As the temperature in a contracting blob of gas becomes higher, the gas exerts a pressure that counteracts the inward force of gravity. At this point, perhaps millions of years after the shock wave slammed into the dark cloud, the contraction stops. If the blob of gas has become hot enough at its center to begin thermonuclear fusion of hydrogen into helium, it has become a star. It will remain in this stable state for millions or billions of years.

An interstellar cloud does not always have to be disturbed by a shock wave to form stars, however. Sometimes a cloud may be hot and dense enough to break up and contract spontaneously under its own gravity. Large clouds can break up into numerous cloudlets this way, and this process leads to the formation of star clusters—groups of stars close to each other in space. Often, two stars will form very close to one another, orbiting around a common center of gravity. This two-star system is called a binary star. Both star clusters and binary stars are more common than single stars.

Until recently, astronomers thought the collision of two stars forming a new star occurred very rarely in the universe. By the beginning of the twenty-first century, however, they had gathered enough observational

▼ **Words to Know**

Binary star: Double-star system in which two stars orbit each other around a central point of gravity.

Black hole: Remains of a massive star that has burned out its nuclear fuel and collapsed under tremendous gravitational force into a single point of infinite mass and gravity.

Core: The central region of a star, where thermonuclear fusion reactions take place that produce the energy necessary for the star to support itself against its own gravity.

Interstellar medium: Space between the stars, consisting mainly of empty space with a very small concentration of gas atoms and tiny solid particles.

Nebula: Cloud of interstellar gas and dust.

Neutron star: Extremely dense, compact, neutron-filled remains of a star following a supernova.

Nuclear fusion: Merging of two or more hydrogen nuclei into one helium nucleus, accompanied by a tremendous release of energy.

Pulsar: Rapidly spinning, blinking neutron star.

Red giant: Stage in which an average-sized star spends the final 10 percent of its lifetime; its surface temperature drops and its diameter expands to 10 to 1,000 times that of the Sun.

Star cluster: Groups of stars close to each other in space that appear to have roughly similar characteristics and, therefore, a common origin.

Supernova: Explosion of a massive star at the end of is lifetime, causing it to shine more brightly than the rest of the stars in the galaxy put together.

White dwarf: Cooling, shrunken core remaining after an average-sized star ceases to burn.

information to know that such collisions are not uncommon within dense clusters of stars. These new stars, called "blue stars," contain more hydrogen than smaller stars, but burn hotter and burn out more quickly. They result from the collision of two (or even three) small, old stars in globular clusters (a tight cluster of tens of thousands to one million very old stars). Astronomers estimate that several hundred such collisions occur every hour. With 100 billion galaxies in the observable universe and each galaxy containing an average of 30 globular clusters, most of the collisions occur far away from the Earth. Over the lifetime (about 10 billion years) of our home galaxy, the Milky Way, astronomers believe there have been at least 1 million collisions within its globular clusters, or about 1 every 10,000 years.

Internal structure of a star

Stars generate energy in their cores, their central and hottest part. The Sun's core has a temperature of about 27,000,000°F (15,000,000°C), and this is hot enough for thermonuclear fusion reactions to take place. Accompanying the transformation of hydrogen to helium is an enormous release of energy, which streams out from the star's core and supplies the energy needed to heat the star's gas. The Sun converts about 600 million tons of hydrogen into helium every second, yet it is so massive that it has

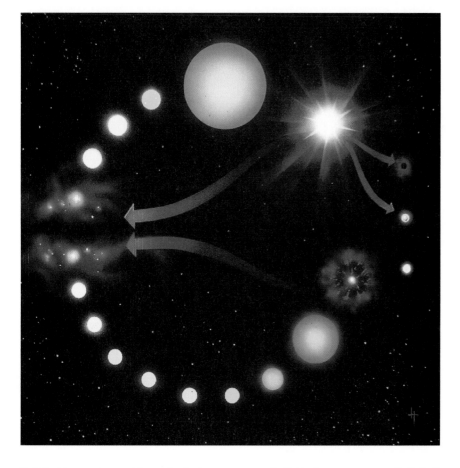

Artwork of the main stages in the life of a star. The lower track shows the evolution of stars like our sun. After it has used all its hydrogen fuel, its helium core becomes a white dwarf. The more massive star on the upper track becomes a red supergiant before exploding in a supernova and leaving behind a black hole or neutron star. *(Reproduced by permission of Photo Researchers, Inc.)*

been maintaining this rate of fuel consumption for five billion years—and will continue to do so for another five billion years.

In the majority of stars, the energy created at the core is carried close to the surface by slow-moving gas currents. As these currents or cells reach the surface atmosphere, they release this energy, which is radiated into space as visible light and other forms of radiation of the electromagnetic spectrum. Once cooled, the currents fall back toward the core where they become heated and rise once again. This organized churning is called convection.

Antares (Alpha Scorpionis) is the bright star dominating this photograph. It is the brightest star in the constellation Scorpius. The bright object to the right of Antares is the M4 (NGC 6121) globular star cluster. *(Reproduced by permission of Photo Researchers, Inc.)*

A star's mass (the total amount of matter in contains) directly influences its size, temperature, and luminosity, or rate of energy output (brightness). The more massive a star is, the stronger its gravity. Mass therefore determines how strong the gravitational force is at every point within the star. This in turn dictates how fast the star has to consume its fuel to keep its gas hot enough to maintain stability everywhere inside it. This controls the temperature structure of the star and the methods by which energy is transported from the core to the surface. It even controls the star's lifetime, since the rate of fuel consumption determines lifetime.

The smallest stars are about 0.08 times the mass of the Sun. If a ball of gas is any smaller than that, its internal temperature will not be high enough to ignite the necessary fusion reactions in its core. It would instead be a brown dwarf, a small, dark, cool ball of dust and gas that never quite becomes a star. The largest stars are about 50 times more massive than the Sun. A star more massive than that would shine so intensely that its radiation would start to overcome gravity; the star would shed mass from its surface so quickly that it could never be stable.

Star deaths

All stars eventually exhaust their hydrogen fuel. At this point, the gas pressure within the star goes down and the star begins to contract under its own gravity. The fate awaiting a star at this point is determined by its mass.

An average-sized star like the Sun will spend the final 10 percent of its life as a red giant. In this phase of a star's evolution, the star's surface temperature drops to between 3,140 and 6,741°F (1,727 and 3,727°C) and its diameter expands to 10 to 1,000 times that of the Sun. The star takes on a reddish color, which is what gives it its name.

Buried deep inside the star is a hot, dense core, about the size of Earth. Helium left burning at the core eventually ejects the star's atmosphere, which floats off into space as a planetary nebula (a cloud of gas and dust). The remaining glowing core is called a white dwarf. Like a dying ember in a campfire, it will gradually cool off and fade into blackness. Space is littered with such dead suns.

A star up to three times the mass of the Sun explodes in a supernova, shedding much of its mass. Any remaining matter of such a star ends up as a densely packed neutron star or pulsar, a rapidly rotating neutron star that emits varying radio waves at precise intervals.

A star more than three times the mass of the Sun will also explode in a supernova. Its remaining mass becomes so concentrated that it shrinks to an indefinitely small size and its gravity becomes completely overpowering. This single point in space where pressure and density are infinite is called a black hole.

[*See also* **Binary star; Black hole; Brown dwarf; Constellation; Galaxy; Gamma-ray burst; Gravity and gravitation; Neutron star; Nova; Nuclear fusion; Orbit; Red giant; Solar system; Starburst galaxy; Star cluster; Stellar magnetic fields; Sun; Supernova; Variable stars; White dwarf**]

Starburst galaxy

Starburst galaxies are galaxies that are in the process of creating massive formations of stars. This type of galaxy emits large amounts of infrared light created by the explosions that happen during the formation of stars. Starburst galaxies were first identified by this incredible amount of infrared light. Infrared light is the portion of the electromagnetic spectrum with wavelengths slightly longer than optical light that takes the form of heat.

Development of starburst galaxies

Astronomers are still searching for why starburst galaxies form. Currently, the most widely accepted theory is a collision or a close encounter

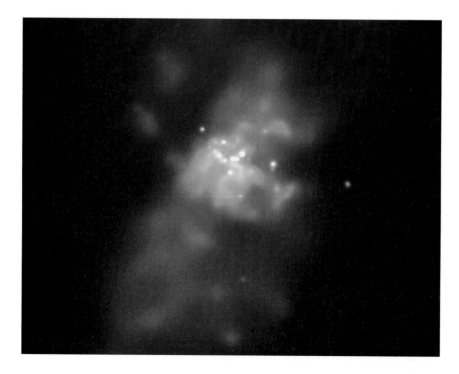

The starburst galaxy Chandra (M82) is 11 million light-years from Earth. (*Reproduced by permission of The Corbis Corporation [Bellevue].*)

Words to Know

Galaxy: A large collection of stars and clusters of stars containing anywhere from a few million to a few trillion stars.

Infrared light: Portion of the electromagnetic spectrum with wavelengths slightly longer than optical light that takes the form of heat.

Milky Way: The galaxy in which our solar system is located.

Supernova: The explosion of a massive star at the end of its lifetime, causing it to shine more brightly than the rest of the stars in the galaxy put together.

with another galaxy that starts a chain reaction. The impact of such a collision produces shock waves throughout the galaxy that push on vast clouds of interstellar dust and gas that are present. These shock waves in turn cause the clouds to collapse and produce short-lived, massive stars. The stars that form from this collision quickly use up their nuclear fuel and explode in a supernova (an extremely bright new star). This explosion produces yet more shock waves and consequently more star formations. The formation of a starburst galaxy ends when its giant clouds of gas are used up or pushed too far away due to the explosions.

Starburst galaxies often emit three-quarters of their light in the form of infrared light. During the formation of stars, the large clouds of gas and dust that the stars form in heat up and the dust emits infrared light, which is able to get through the clouds of gas. But because the light that comes through is infrared, starburst galaxies are relatively unspectacular when viewed through a regular telescope. However, an infrared telescope (a telescope that allows the user to see the usually invisible infrared wavelengths) shows starburst galaxies standing out from all other galaxies because of their brightness from the continuing formation of stars.

Starburst galaxies most often appear irregularly shaped when compared to regular galaxies. Most galaxies are spiral or elliptical in shape. For instance, both the Milky Way galaxy (our galaxy that includes a few hundred billion stars, the Sun, and our solar system) and the Andromeda galaxy (the nearest galaxy similar in size to the Milky Way, located 2.2 million light-years away) are spiral-shaped. Astronomers believe that the irregular shape of starburst galaxies is due to their collision or near-collision with other galaxies.

Infrared Astronomical Satellite and the Hubble Space Telescope

Because the study of infrared radiation is limited from Earth's surface (water and carbon dioxide in Earth's atmosphere block most of it), astronomers had a limited knowledge of starburst galaxies. This changed when an infrared telescope was mounted onto a satellite observatory that was sent into space in 1983. Three countries—the United States, England, and the Netherlands—combined their efforts to develop and launch the Infrared Astronomical Satellite (IRAS). The IRAS was equipped with an infrared telescope that observed, among other things, that thousands of starburst galaxies exist in space. It also showed that starburst galaxies consist of nearly one-third of the energy in the universe, suggesting that starburst galaxies are the main source of new stars.

Another high-tech space observatory was launched in 1990. The Hubble Space Telescope (HST) was sent into space and acted as an observatory for astronomers from dozens of countries. With its high-resolution camera sending back sharp pictures to Earth, the HST showed that violent star formations—typically thought to occur only in distant galaxies—also occurred in the closest starburst galaxy (about 1,000 light-years from Earth). The HST also confirmed the theory that stars are often born in dense clusters (close groupings) within starburst galaxies.

[*See also* **Galaxy; Infrared astronomy; Star**]

Star cluster

Star clusters are groups of stars close to each other in space that appear to have roughly similar characteristics and, therefore, a common origin.

Some of the over 100 billion stars in the Milky Way, our home galaxy, are grouped together in either tight or loose star clusters. More than 100 tight groupings, called globular clusters, surround the galaxy's spiral arms in a great halo. Loose groupings, called open clusters or galactic clusters, are far more numerous and are found toward the center of the galaxy.

Globular clusters radiate with a continuous glow. These nearly spherical (ball-shaped) star systems contain anywhere from tens of thousands to one million stars. They are most heavily concentrated at the center of the cluster.

The Pleiades open star cluster (M45), situated in the constellation Taurus. The Pleiades cluster is about 400 light-years from Earth and is young (only about 50 million years old) on a galactic time scale. *(Reproduced by permission of Photo Researchers, Inc.)*

Words to Know

Cluster of galaxies: A group of galaxies that are bound together by gravity.

Galaxy: A large collection of stars and clusters of stars containing anywhere from a few million to a few trillion stars.

Globular cluster: A tight cluster of tens of thousands to one million very old stars.

Light-year: The distance light travels in one year in the vacuum of space—roughly 5.9 trillion miles (9.5 trillion kilometers).

Open cluster: A loose cluster of roughly a few hundred young stars.

Supercluster: A connected group of clusters of galaxies that may extend for hundreds of millions of light-years.

Void: Region of space extending for hundreds of millions of light-years that contains few if any galaxies.

While in reality there is a great distance between stars in these clusters, an observer on Earth may find it impossible to pick out individual stars.

In contrast to globular clusters, which are 10 to 13 billion years old, open clusters are quite young. These groups, formed just a few million to a few billion years ago, contain hot young stars and some stars still in formation. Open clusters have far fewer members than globular clusters (usually just a few hundred) and have no particular shape.

Over 1,000 open clusters have been identified in our galaxy. However, many more may be undetected because of interstellar matter that blocks our view of the Milky Way's plane. One the most famous of the open clusters is the Pleiades (pronounced PLEE-a-deez), or the Seven Sisters. This grouping in the Taurus constellation consists of six or seven stars visible to the naked eye, but many more when viewed through a telescope.

Superclusters

Superclusters are currently the largest structures known in the universe. As stars and clusters of stars group together into galaxies, galaxies collect into groups known as clusters of galaxies. On a larger scale, superclusters are clusters of clusters of galaxies. As clusters of galaxies group into superclusters they leave empty spaces called voids between the superclusters. Superclusters and voids typically extend for hundreds of millions of light-years.

Beyond the Milky Way

Star clusters are certainly not limited to the Milky Way galaxy. In 1924, U.S. astronomer Edwin Hubble identified globular clusters in what, at the time, were believed to be nebula (clouds of dust particles and hydrogen gas) within the Milky Way. He discovered that the distance from Earth to these globulars, and the nebula in which they were located, was so great that these globulars had to be entirely separate galaxies. Thus, Hubble proved that the Milky Way was not the only galaxy in the universe.

[See also **Star**]

Statistics

Statistics is that branch of mathematics devoted to the collection, compilation, display, and interpretation of numerical data. The term statistics actually has two quite different meanings. In one case, it can refer to any set of numbers that has been collected and then arranged in some format that makes them easy to read and understand. In the second case, the term refers to a variety of mathematical procedures used to determine what those data may mean, if anything.

An example of the first kind of statistic is the data on female African Americans in various age groups, shown in Table 1. The table summarizes some interesting information but does not, in and of itself, seem to have any particular meaning. An example of the second kind of statistic is the data collected during the test of a new drug, shown in Table 2. This table not only summarizes information collected in the experiment, but also, presumably, can be used to determine the effectiveness of the drug.

Populations and samples

Two fundamental concepts used in statistical analysis are population and sample. The term population refers to a complete set of individuals, objects, or events that belong to some category. For example, all of the players who are employed by major league baseball teams make up the population of professional major league baseball players. The term sample refers to some subset of a population that is representative of the

Words to Know

Deviation: The difference between any one measurement and the mean of the set of scores.

Histogram: A bar graph that shows the frequency distribution of a variable by means of solid bars without any space between them.

Mean: A measure of central tendency found by adding all the numbers in a set and dividing by the number of numbers.

Measure of central tendency: Average.

Measure of variability: A general term for any method of measuring the spread of measurements around some measure of central tendency.

Median: The middle value in a set of measurements when those measurements are arranged in sequence from least to greatest.

Mode: The value that occurs most frequently in any set of measurements.

Normal curve: A frequency distribution curve with a symmetrical, bell-shaped appearance.

Population: A complete set of individuals, objects, or events that belong to some category.

Range: The difference between the largest and smallest numbers in a set of observations.

Sample: A subset of actual observations taken from any larger set of possible observations.

total population. For example, one might go down the complete list of all major league baseball players and select every tenth name on the list. That subset of every tenth name would then make up a sample of all professional major league baseball players.

Samples are important in statistical studies because it is almost never possible to collect data from all members in a population. For example, suppose one would like to know how many professional baseball players are Republicans and how many are Democrats. One way to answer that question would be to ask that question of every professional baseball player. However, it might be difficult to get in touch with every player and to get every player to respond. The larger the population, the more difficult it is to get data from every member of the population.

Most statistical studies, therefore, select a sample of individuals from a population to interview. One could use, for example the every-tenth-name list mentioned above to collect data about the political parties to which baseball players belong. That approach would be easier and less expensive than contacting everyone in the population.

The problem with using samples, however, is to be certain that the members of the sample are typical of the members of the population as a whole. If someone decided to interview only those baseball players who live in New York City, for example, the sample would not be a good one. People who live in New York City may have very different political concerns than people who live in the rest of the country.

One of the most important problems in any statistical study, then, is to collect a fair sample from a population. That fair sample is called a random sample because it is arranged in such a way that everyone in the population has an equal chance of being selected. Statisticians have now developed a number of techniques for selecting random samples for their studies.

Displaying data

Once data have been collected on some particular subject, those data must be displayed in some format that makes it easy for readers to see and understand. Table 1 makes it very easy for anyone who wants to know the number of female African Americans in any particular age group.

In general, the most common methods for displaying data are tables and charts or graphs. One of the most common types of graphs used is the display of data as a histogram. A histogram is a bar graph in which each bar represents some particular variable, and the height of each bar represents the number of cases of that variable. For example, one could make a histogram of the information in Table 1 by drawing six bars, one representing each of the six age groups shown in the table. The height of each bar would correspond to the number of individuals in each age group. The bar farthest to the left, representing the age group 0 to 19, would be much higher than any other bar because there are more individuals in that age group than in any other. The bar second from the right would be the shortest because it represents the age group with the fewest numbers of individuals.

Another way to represent data is called a frequency distribution curve. Suppose that the data in Table 1 were arranged so that the number of female African Americans for every age were represented. The table would have to show the number of individuals 1 year of age, those 2 years

Table 1. Number of Female African Americans in Various Age Groups

Age	Number
0–19	5,382,025
20–29	2,982,305
30–39	2,587,550
40–49	1,567,735
50–59	1,335,235
60+	1,606,335

Table 2. Statistics

	Improved	Not Improved	Total
Experimental group	62	38	100
Control group	45	55	100
Total	107	93	200

of age, those 3 years of age, and so on to the oldest living female African American. One could also make a histogram of these data. But a more efficient way would be to draw a line graph with each point on the graph standing for the number of individuals of each age. Such a graph would be called a frequency distribution curve because it shows the frequency (number of cases) for each different category (age group, in this case).

Many phenomena produce distribution curves that have a very distinctive shape, high in the middle and sloping off to either side. These distribution curves are sometimes called "bell curves" because their shape resembles a bell. For example, suppose you record the average weight of 10,000 American 14-year-old boys. You would probably find that the majority of those boys had a weight of perhaps 130 pounds. A smaller number might have weights of 150 or 110 pounds, a still smaller number, weights of 170 or 90 pounds, and very few boys with weights of 190 or 70 pounds. The graph you get for this measurement probably has a peak at the center (around 130 pounds) with downward slopes on either side of the center. This graph would reflect a normal distribution of weights.

Other phenomena do not exhibit normal distributions. At one time in the United States, the grades received by students in high school followed a normal distribution. The most common grade by far was a C, with fewer Bs and Ds, and fewer still As and Fs. In fact, grade distribution has for many years been used as an example of normal distribution.

Today, however, that situation has changed. The majority of grades received by students in high schools tend to be As and Bs, with fewer Cs, Ds and Fs. A distribution that is lopsided on one side or the other of the center of the graph is said to be a skewed distribution.

Measures of central tendency

Once a person has collected a mass of data, these data can be manipulated by a great variety of statistical techniques. Some of the most familiar of these techniques fall under the category of measures of central tendency. By measures of central tendency, we mean what the average of a set of data is. The problem is that the term average can have different meanings—mean, median, and mode among them.

In order to understand the differences of these three measures, consider a classroom consisting of only six students. A study of the six students shows that their family incomes are as follows: $20,000; $25,000; $20,000; $30,000; $27,500; and $150,000. What is the average income for the students in this classroom?

The measure of central tendency that most students learn in school is the mean. The mean for any set of numbers is found by adding all the numbers and dividing by the number of numbers. In this example, the mean would be equal to $20,000 + $25,000 + $20,000 + $30,000 + $27,500 + $150,000 ÷ 6 = $45,417.

But how much useful information does this answer give about the six students in the classroom? The mean that has been calculated ($45,417) is greater than the household income of five of the six students. Another way of calculating central tendency is known as the median. The median value of a set of measurements is the middle value when the measurements are arranged in order from least to greatest. When there are an even number of measurements, the median is half way between the middle two measurements. In the above example, the measurements can be rearranged from least to greatest: $20,000; $20,000; $25,000; $27,500; $30,000; $150,000. In this case, the middle two measurements are $25,000 and $27,500, and half way between them is $26,250, the median in this case. You can see that the median in this example gives a better view of the household incomes for the classroom than does the mean.

A third measure of central tendency is the mode. The mode is the value most frequently observed in a study. In the household income study, the mode is $20,000 since it is the value found most often in the study.

Each measure of central tendency has certain advantages and disadvantages and is used, therefore, under certain special circumstances.

Measures of variability

Suppose that a teacher gave the same test four different times to two different classes and obtained the following results: Class 1: 80 percent, 80 percent, 80 percent, 80 percent, 80 percent; Class 2: 60 percent, 70 percent, 80 percent, 90 percent, 100 percent. If you calculate the mean for both sets of scores, you get the same answer: 80 percent. But the collection of scores from which this mean was obtained was very different in the two cases. The way that statisticians have of distinguishing cases such as this is known as measuring the variability of the sample. As with measures of central tendency, there are a number of ways of measuring the variability of a sample.

Probably the simplest method for measuring variability is to find the range of the sample, that is, the difference between the largest and smallest observation. The range of measurements in Class 1 is 0, and the range in class 2 is 40 percent. Simply knowing that fact gives a much better understanding of the data obtained from the two classes. In class 1, the mean was 80 percent, and the range was 0, but in class 2, the mean was 80 percent, and the range was 40 percent.

Other measures of variability are based on the difference between any one measurement and the mean of the set of scores. This measure is known as the deviation. As you can imagine, the greater the difference among measurements, the greater the variability. In the case of Class 2 above, the deviation for the first measurement is 20 percent (80 percent − 60 percent), and the deviation for the second measurement is 10 percent (80 percent − 70 percent).

Probably the most common measures of variability used by statisticians are called the variance and standard deviation. Variance is defined as the mean of the squared deviations of a set of measurements. Calculating the variance is a somewhat complicated task. One has to find each of the deviations in the set of measurements, square each one, add all the squares, and divide by the number of measurements. In the example above, the variance would be equal to $[(20)^2 + (10)^2 + (0)^2 + (10)^2 + (20)^2]$ $\div 5 = 200$.

For a number of reasons, the variance is used less often in statistics than is the standard deviation. The standard deviation is the square root of the variance, in this case, $\sqrt{200} = 14.1$. The standard deviation is useful because in any normal distribution, a large fraction of the measurements (about 68 percent) are located within one standard deviation of the mean. Another 27 percent (for a total of 95 percent of all measurements) lie within two standard deviations of the mean.

Other statistical tests

Many other kinds of statistical tests have been invented to find out the meaning of data. Look at the data presented in Table 2. Those data were collected in an experiment to see if a new kind of drug was effective in curing a disease. The people in the experimental group received the drug, while those in the control group received a placebo, a pill that looked like the drug but contained nothing more than starch. The table shows the number of people who got better ("Improved") and those who didn't ("Not Improved") in each group. Was the drug effective in curing the disease?

You might try to guess the answer to that question just by looking at the table. But is the 62 number in the Experimental Group really significantly greater than the 45 in the Control Group? Statisticians use the term significant to indicate that some result has occurred more often than might be expected purely on the basis of chance alone.

Statistical tests have been developed to answer this question mathematically. In this example, the test is based on the fact that each group was made up of 100 people. Purely on the basis of chance alone, then, one might expect 50 people in each group to get better and 50 not to get better. If the data show results different from that distribution, the results could have been caused by the new drug.

The mathematical problem, then, is to compare the 62 observed in the first cell with the 50 expected, the 38 observed in the second cell with the 50 expected, the 45 observed in the third cell with the 50 expected, and the 55 observed in the fourth cell with the 50 expected.

At first glance, it would appear that the new medication was at least partially successful since the number of those who took it and improved (62) was greater than the number who took it and did not improve (38). But a type of statistical test called a chi square test will give a more precise answer. The chi square test involves comparing the observed frequencies in Table 2 with a set of expected frequencies that can be calculated from the number of individuals taking the tests. The value of chi square calculated can then be compared to values in a table to see how likely the results were due to chance or to some real effect of the medication.

Another common technique used for analyzing numerical data is called the correlation coefficient. The correlation coefficient shows how closely two variables are related to each other. For example, many medical studies have attempted to determine the connection between smoking and lung cancer. The question is whether heavy smokers are more likely to develop lung cancer.

One way to do such studies is to measure the amount of smoking a person has done in her or his lifetime and compare the rate of lung cancer among those individuals. A mathematical formula allows the researcher to calculate the correlation coefficient between these two sets of data—rate of smoking and risk for lung cancer. That coefficient can range between 1.0, meaning the two are perfectly correlated, and −1.0, meaning the two have an inverse relationship (when one is high, the other is low).

The correlation test is a good example of the limitations of statistical analysis. Suppose that the correlation coefficient in the example above turned out to be 1.0. That number would mean that people who smoke the most are always the most likely to develop lung cancer. But what the correlation coefficient does *not* say is what the cause and effect relationship, if any, might be. It does *not* say that smoking *causes* cancer.

Chi square and correlation coefficient are only two of dozens of statistical tests now available for use by researchers. The specific kinds of data collected and the kinds of information a researcher wants to obtain from these data determine the specific test to be used.

Steam engine

A steam engine is a machine that converts the heat energy of steam into mechanical energy. A steam engine passes its steam into a cylinder, where it then pushes a piston back and forth. It is with this piston movement that the engine can do mechanical work. The steam engine was the major power source of the Industrial Revolution in Europe in the eighteenth and nineteenth centuries. It dominated industry and transportation for 150 years.

History

The first steam-powered machine was built in 1698 by the English military engineer Thomas Savery (c. 1650–1715). His invention, designed to pump water out of coal mines, was known as the Miner's Friend. The machine, which had no moving parts, consisted of a simple boiler—a steam chamber whose valves were located on the surface—and a pipe leading to the water in the mine below. Water was heated in the boiler chamber until its steam filled the chamber, forcing out any remaining

Words to Know

Condenser: An instrument for cooling air or gases.

Cylinder: The chamber of an engine in which the piston moves.

Piston: A sliding piece that is moved by or moves against fluid pressure within a cylindrical vessel or chamber.

Turbine: An engine that moves in a circular motion when force, such as moving water, is applied to its series of baffles (thin plates or screens) radiating from a central shaft.

water or air. The valves were then closed and cold water was sprayed over the chamber. This chilled and condensed the steam inside to form a vacuum. When the valves were reopened, the vacuum sucked up the water from the mine, and the process could then be repeated.

A few years later, an English engineer and partner of Savery named Thomas Newcomen (1663–1729) improved the steam pump. He increased efficiency by setting a moving piston inside a cylinder, a technique still in use today. A cylinder—a long, thin, closed chamber separate from the boiler—replaced the large, open boiler chamber. A piston—a sliding piece that fits in the cylinder—was used to create motion instead of a vacuum. Steam filled the cylinder from an open valve. When filled, the cylinder was sprayed with water, causing the steam inside to condense into water and create a partial vacuum. The pressure of the outside air then forced the piston down, producing a power stroke. The piston was connected to a beam, which was connected to a water pump at the bottom of the mine by a pump-rod. Through these connections, the movement of the piston caused the water pump to suck up the water.

Watt's breakthrough

The most important improvement in steam engine design was brought about by the Scottish engineer James Watt (1736–1819). He set out to improve the performance of Newcomen's engine and by 1769 had arrived at the conclusion: if the steam were condensed separately from the cylinder, the cylinder could always be kept hot. That year he introduced the design of a steam engine that had a separate condenser and sealed cylinders. Since this kept the heating and cooling processes separate, his machine could work constantly, without any long pause at each cycle to reheat the cylinder. Watt's refined steam engine design used one-third less fuel than a comparable Newcomen engine.

Over the next fifteen years, Watt continued to improve his engine and made three significant additions. He introduced the centrifugal governor, a device that could control steam output and engine speed. He made the engine double-acting by allowing steam to enter alternately on either side of the piston. This allowed the engine to work rapidly and deliver power on the downward as well as on the upward piston stroke. Most important, he attached a flywheel to the engine.

Flywheels allow the engine to run more smoothly by creating a more constant load, and they convert the conventional back-and-forth power stroke into a circular (rotary) motion that can be adapted more readily to power machinery. By 1790, Watt's improved steam engine offered a powerful, reliable power source that could be located almost anywhere. It was used to pump bellows for blast furnaces, to power huge hammers

Trains powered by steam engines. *(Reproduced by permission of Corbis-Bettmann.)*

for shaping and strengthening forged metals, and to turn machinery at textile mills. More than anything, it was Watt's steam engine that speeded up the Industrial Revolution both in England and the rest of the world.

High-pressure engines

The next advance in steam engine technology involved the realization that steam itself, rather than the condensing of steam to create a vacuum, could power an engine. In 1804, American inventor Oliver Evans (1755–1819) designed the first high-pressure, non-condensing engine. The engine, which was stationary, operated at 30 revolutions per minute and was used to power a marble-cutting saw. The high-pressure engines used large cylindrical tanks of water heated from beneath to produce steam.

Steam was successfully adapted to power boats in 1802 and railways in 1829. Later, some of the first automobiles were powered by steam. In the 1880s, the English engineer Charles A. Parsons (1854–1931) produced the first steam turbine. By 1900, the steam engine had evolved into a highly sophisticated and powerful engine that propelled huge ships on the oceans and ran turbogenerators that supplied electricity.

Once the dominant power source, steam engines eventually declined in popularity as other power sources became available. Although there were more than 60,000 steam cars made in the United States between 1897 and 1927, the steam engine eventually gave way to the internal-combustion engine as a power source for vehicles.

[*See also* **Diesel engine; Internal-combustion engine; Jet engine**]

Stellar magnetic fields

Stellar magnetic fields are an assortment of powerful forces that can be observed at the surfaces of and surrounding stars like the Sun. Astronomers have yet to obtain a complete understanding of the magnetic fields of stars, but they continue to observe their activity in the hopes of understanding their effects on a star's interior makeup, atmosphere, rotation, and future evolution.

The mysterious magnetic field

A typical magnet—such as one commonly found on a refrigerator—is called a dipolar magnet. Dipolar refers to the two areas of the magnet from which it receives its power: opposing north and south poles. A star's

Words to Know

Convection zone: Outermost one-third of the Sun's interior where heat is transferred from the core toward the surface via slow-moving gas currents.

Spectropolarimeter: A device that gathers information on the polarization state of individual chemical reactions from a star; these reactions are seen as lines in the star's spectrum.

Sunspot: A region of the Sun where the temperature is lower than that of the surrounding surface region and consequently appears darker. The presence of a strong, concentrated magnetic field produces the cooling effect.

Zeeman-Doppler imaging: The process of using a spectropolarimeter to measure the Zeeman effect.

Zeeman effect: A change in the spectral lines—their shape and polarization—caused by the magnetic field of the Sun.

magnetic field works in basically the same way, but it is much more complex. How stellar magnetic fields originate remains a mystery among astrophysicists. In space, there is no naturally occurring magnetic iron, yet astronomers know that magnetism does exist in space.

The most studied stellar magnetic field

The Sun, the only star our solar system, has show that it has a magnetic field that reaches all over its surface. Astronomers know that this magnetic field affects the rotation of the Sun and the movement of chemical elements around its surface. It has concentrated areas of magnetism called sunspots (dark areas on the Sun that produce magnetic storms).

While astronomers remain uncertain of exactly how the Sun's magnetic fields work, the most widely accepted theory involves a stellar dynamo. A stellar dynamo can be thought of like a generator (an engine usually fueled by gas that spins a magnet wrapped in coil, producing electricity). Astronomers theorize that in the case of the Sun, instead of producing electricity, the stellar dynamo generates a magnetic field in two ways, each involving powerful motions. The first involves the movement of gases in the convection zone. (A convection zone is the upper layer of a star.) In this zone, material close to the surface of a star rises as heat moves outward from the lower layers of the surface. This process results in hot gas rising from the surface, in a way that is similar to hot air rising on Earth. Upon the release of the heat of the gas at the Sun's surface, the gas drops down again as it replaced by the hotter gases below the surface.

The second type of motion in a stellar dynamo is a result of the Sun being made of gas (mainly hydrogen and helium). When the Sun rotates, its speed is varied due to its gassy composition; this differs from planets, whose solid composition produces a regular rotation. The irregular rotation of the Sun is called differential rotation. It causes the equator (the middle of the Sun) to spin faster than the poles (the top and bottom of the Sun).

Interiors of binary star system Gliese 752. *(Reproduced by permission of The Corbis Corporation [Bellevue].)*

Astronomers believe that the combination of the two stellar dynamo motions—involving convection zone gases and differential rotation—gen-

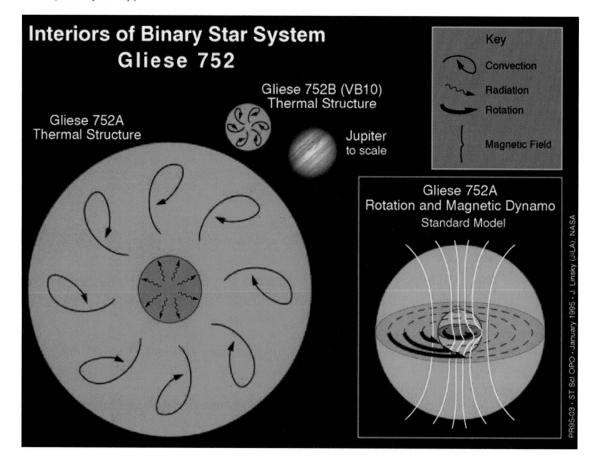

erate the Sun's magnetic field. Continued observations of the Sun and other stars will help confirm this theory or bring forward other possibilities about how stellar magnetic fields are generated.

Methods used to study stellar magnetic fields

Astronomers study stellar magnetic fields by using a method known as the Zeeman effect. In this method, spectral lines are studied. Spectral lines are lights of a single frequency (wavelength) that are emitted by an atom when an electron changes its energy level. Chemical reactions in stars produce lines of varying intensities along a spectrum, thereby allowing scientists to recognize their chemical makeup. The Zeeman effect is a change in the spectral lines—their shape and polarization (a process that causes light waves to create a specific pattern)—caused by the magnetic field of the Sun.

Another method that astronomers use to study stellar magnetic fields is called Zeeman-Doppler imaging (ZDI). ZDI is the process of using a spectropolarimeter to measure the Zeeman effect of stars. A spectropolarimeter is a device that analyzes the polarization state of chemical reactions from stars; these reactions are viewed as spectral lines. Using this method, scientists can detect and map the surface magnetic field of active stars that range in age from a few million to more than ten billion years old.

Importance of stellar magnetic fields

Astronomers are still uncertain of the origins of stellar magnetic fields. But with continued observations, they believe they will learn more about the large and small structures of magnetic fields that should help them comprehend how and where those fields originate and how they affect the interiors and atmospheres of stars. Understanding stellar magnetic fields will help astronomers learn more not only about the physical makeup of stars, but about their future evolution, as well.

[*See also* **Star; Sun**]

Storm surge

A storm surge is a rise in water level caused by a combination of wind and low atmospheric pressure. It is the most destructive force of a hurricane (an intense cyclone that forms over warm tropical oceans; called a typhoon when it occurs in the western Pacific Ocean and adjacent seas)

Words to Know

Atmospheric pressure: The pressure exerted by the atmosphere at Earth's surface due to the weight of the air.

Hurricane: A severe swirling tropical storm with heavy rains and winds exceeding 74 miles (119 kilometers) per hour.

Tide: The periodic variation in the surface level of the oceans, seas, and bays caused by the gravitation attraction of the Moon (and to a lesser extent the Sun).

Formation of a storm surge

When a hurricane is forming over open, warm ocean waters, the wind pushing the water and the low atmospheric pressure in the eye of the hurricane cause the level of the sea to rise, whipping the water into gigantic waves. Because this is happening away from land, the water can escape and move freely away from the building storm. But as the hurricane moves towards land and the depth of the water becomes more shallow, the ever-increasing wall of water does not have a chance to flow away. Instead it is built up around the eye of the hurricane and forms huge waves. These mountainous waves pound against the land and anything in its path—buildings, homes, piers, and people. Storm surges can be more devastating depending upon the strength of the hurricane's winds and the shallowness of the off-shore waters.

Storm tide

A storm surge can also become much more destructive if it occurs during high tide (an increase in water level due to the Moon's gravitational pull on Earth). This is called a storm tide. For example, if a normal high tide for a particular area is three feet and a storm surge occurs at the same time with fifteen-foot waves, a storm tide with eighteen-foot waves is formed. This occurrence makes the storm surge even more devastating.

Storm surge destruction

Storm surges have long been recognized as the most destructive part of a hurricane. Causing drownings and property destruction, this incredible wall of water stops for nothing in its path. As it moves across the land, it picks up and carries with it debris that it finds along the way, such as cars, utility poles, and boats. A hurricane hit Galveston, Texas, in 1900 and killed 6,000. The storm surge from the "Great Galveston Hurricane" formed waves that were twenty-five feet high. In 1970, the Bay of Bengal in Bangladesh suffered through a hurricane that produced a storm surge with thirty-foot-high waves that killed approximately 200,000 people.

Prevention of damage

After suffering through such incredible devastation, the city of Galveston completed the building of a seawall four years later. A little over three miles long and seventeen feet above average low tide mark, the Galveston seawall would act as a line of defense by interfering in the progress of the storm surge's attack on the land and by catching some of the destructive debris that it carries along its way. The city of Galveston

A storm surge flooded this trailer park in Islamorada, Florida, during Hurricane Irene. *(Reproduced by permission of The Corbis Corporation [Bellevue].)*

also actually raised the level of the city after devoting ten years to the project. The entire city—every church, home, and business—had 14 million cubic yards (10.7 million cubic meters) of sand poured in underneath it. The combination of building a seawall and raising the level of the city helped increase the odds of Galveston successfully surviving a storm surge. The investment in prevention paid off: On August 16, 1915, a hurricane of almost the same force as the 1900 storm hit the city. While the 1915 hurricane was still tragic—about a dozen people lost their lives— the number of deaths was far below the 6,000 in 1900.

[*See also* **Cyclone and anticyclone**]

Stress

Stress is mental or physical tension brought about by internal or external pressures. The feeling of stress may be mild or severe and it can last a short time or over a longer period. Many events may cause stress. They range from everyday occurrences such as taking a test or driving through rush-hour traffic to more traumatic experiences such as the death of a loved one or a serious illness.

Stress may be a factor in causing disease. Researchers believe that stress disrupts the body's homeostasis or balanced state, which leads to a weakening of the body's immune system. Chronic (frequently occurring) stress can thus bring about serious illnesses.

People who experience severe traumas, such as soldiers during combat, may develop a condition called post-traumatic stress disorder (PTSD). This condition was called shell shock during World War I (1914–18) and battle fatigue during World War II (1939–45). Sufferers of PTSD experience depression, nightmares, feelings of guilt for having survived, and flashbacks to the traumatic events. They may be excessively sensitive to noise and may even become violent.

Until the twenty-first century, scientists believed humans and animals reacted to stress in a common manner, by preparing to do battle or to flee. This syndrome is known as "fight or flight." In 2000, however, a group of researchers issued a report asserting that females (both human and animal) often show a different reaction to stress. Instead of aggression and escape, their reaction is one of nurturing and seeking the support of others. The researchers believe this response, called "tend and be-friend," is the result of either hormonal differences between the sexes or learning and cultural conditioning experienced long ago in our evolu-

▼ Words to Know

Adrenaline: Chemical released from the adrenal gland in response to stress, exercise, or strong emotions.

Atherosclerosis: Disease of the arteries in which fatty material accumulates on the inner walls of the arteries, obstructing the flow of blood.

Homeostasis: State of being in balance.

Post-traumatic stress disorder (PTSD): Condition developed as a response to traumatic events such as those experienced in combat.

tionary history. When human were first evolving, the "tend-and-befriend" response would have reduced the risk to females and their offspring posed by predators, natural disasters, and other threats.

Stress and illness

Some of the physical signs of stress are a dry mouth and throat; tight muscles in the neck, shoulders, and back; chronic neck and back problems; headaches; indigestion; tremors; muscle tics; insomnia; and fatigue. Emotional signs of stress include tension, anxiety, depression, and emotional exhaustion.

During stress, heart rate quickens, blood pressure increases, and the body releases the hormone adrenaline, which speeds up the body's metabolism. If the stress continues over a period of time and the body does not return to its normal balanced state, the immune system begins to weaken.

Medical researchers have determined that chronic stress causes the accumulation of fat, starch, calcium, and other substances in the linings of the blood vessels. This can lead to atherosclerosis, a condition in which blood flow through the arteries is obstructed. This condition ultimately results in heart disease. Other diseases associated with stress are adult diabetes, ulcers, high blood pressure, asthma, migraine headaches, cancer, and the common cold. While both sexes can suffer greatly from stress, men seem to experience more stress-related illnesses like hypertension and alcohol and drug abuse.

Treatments for stress reduction

Some psychiatrists and therapists treat patients suffering from stress with medications such as antianxiety or antidepressant drugs. Other therapists help patients develop coping strategies to reduce or eliminate stress from their lives. Some life-style changes are often recommended. These include adopting a healthy diet, quitting smoking, increasing exercise activity, developing relaxation techniques (such as deep breathing and meditation), and taking part in group discussions. Knowing the causes of stress and being able to talk about them are considered important for reducing or eliminating stress.

Where to Learn More

Books

Earth Sciences

Cox, Reg, and Neil Morris. *The Natural World.* Philadelphia, PA: Chelsea House, 2000.

Dasch, E. Julius, editor. *Earth Sciences for Students.* Four volumes. New York: Macmillan Reference, 1999.

Denecke, Edward J., Jr. *Let's Review: Earth Science.* Second edition. Hauppauge, NY: Barron's, 2001.

Engelbert, Phillis. *Dangerous Planet: The Science of Natural Disasters.* Three volumes. Farmington Hills, MI: UXL, 2001.

Gardner, Robert. *Human Evolution.* New York: Franklin Watts, 1999.

Hall, Stephen. *Exploring the Oceans.* Milwaukee, WI: Gareth Stevens, 2000.

Knapp, Brian. *Earth Science: Discovering the Secrets of the Earth.* Eight volumes. Danbury, CT: Grolier Educational, 2000.

Llewellyn, Claire. *Our Planet Earth.* New York: Scholastic Reference, 1997.

Moloney, Norah. *The Young Oxford Book of Archaeology.* New York: Oxford University Press, 1997.

Nardo, Don. *Origin of Species: Darwin's Theory of Evolution.* San Diego, CA: Lucent Books, 2001.

Silverstein, Alvin, Virginia Silverstein, and Laura Silverstein Nunn.*Weather and Climate.* Brookfield, CN: Twenty-First Century Books, 1998.

Williams, Bob, Bob Ashley, Larry Underwood, and Jack Herschbach. *Geography.* Parsippany, NJ: Dale Seymour Publications, 1997.

Life Sciences

Barrett, Paul M. *National Geographic Dinosaurs.* Washington, D.C.: National Geographic Society, 2001.

Fullick, Ann. *The Living World.* Des Plaines, IL: Heinemann Library, 1999.

Gamlin, Linda. *Eyewitness: Evolution.* New York: Dorling Kindersley, 2000.

Greenaway, Theresa. *The Plant Kingdom: A Guide to Plant Classification and Biodiversity.* Austin, TX: Raintree Steck-Vaughn, 2000.

Kidd, J. S., and Renee A Kidd. *Life Lines: The Story of the New Genetics.* New York: Facts on File, 1999.

Kinney, Karin, editor. *Our Environment.* Alexandria, VA: Time-Life Books, 2000.

Where to Learn More

Nagel, Rob. *Body by Design: From the Digestive System to the Skeleton.* Two volumes. Farmington Hills, MI: UXL., 2000.

Parker, Steve. *The Beginner's Guide to Animal Autopsy: A "Hands-in" Approach to Zoology, the World of Creatures and What's Inside Them.* Brookfield, CN: Copper Beech Books, 1997.

Pringle, Laurence. *Global Warming: The Threat of Earth's Changing Climate.* New York: SeaStar Books, 2001.

Riley, Peter. *Plant Life.* New York: Franklin Watts, 1999.

Stanley, Debbie. *Genetic Engineering: The Cloning Debate.* New York: Rosen Publishing Group, 2000.

Whyman, Kate. *The Animal Kingdom: A Guide to Vertebrate Classification and Biodiversity.* Austin, TX: Raintree Steck-Vaughn, 1999.

Physical Sciences

Allen, Jerry, and Georgiana Allen. *The Horse and the Iron Ball: A Journey Through Time, Space, and Technology.* Minneapolis, MN: Lerner Publications, 2000.

Berger, Samantha, *Light.* New York: Scholastic, 1999.

Bonnet, Bob L., and Dan Keen. *Physics.* New York: Sterling Publishing, 1999.

Clark, Stuart. *Discovering the Universe.* Milwaukee, WI: Gareth Stevens, 2000.

Fleisher, Paul, and Tim Seeley. *Matter and Energy: Basic Principles of Matter and Thermodynamics.* Minneapolis, MN: Lerner Publishing, 2001.

Gribbin, John. *Eyewitness: Time and Space.* New York: Dorling Kindersley, 2000.

Holland, Simon. *Space.* New York: Dorling Kindersley, 2001.

Kidd, J. S., and Renee A. Kidd. *Quarks and Sparks: The Story of Nuclear Power.* New York: Facts on File, 1999.

Levine, Shar, and Leslie Johnstone. *The Science of Sound and Music.* New York: Sterling Publishing, 2000

Naeye, Robert. *Signals from Space: The Chandra X-ray Observatory.* Austin, TX: Raintree Steck-Vaughn, 2001.

Newmark, Ann. *Chemistry.* New York: Dorling Kindersley, 1999.

Oxlade, Chris. *Acids and Bases.* Chicago, IL: Heinemann Library, 2001.

Vogt, Gregory L. *Deep Space Astronomy.* Brookfield, CT: Twenty-First Century Books, 1999.

Technology and Engineering Sciences

Baker, Christopher W. *Scientific Visualization: The New Eyes of Science.* Brookfield, CT: Millbrook Press, 2000.

Cobb, Allan B. *Scientifically Engineered Foods: The Debate over What's on Your Plate.* New York: Rosen Publishing Group, 2000.

Cole, Michael D. *Space Launch Disaster: When Liftoff Goes Wrong.* Springfield, NJ: Enslow, 2000.

Deedrick, Tami. *The Internet.* Austin, TX: Raintree Steck-Vaughn, 2001.

DuTemple, Leslie A. *Oil Spills.* San Diego, CA: Lucent Books, 1999.

Gaines, Ann Graham. *Satellite Communication.* Mankata, MN: Smart Apple Media, 2000.

Gardner, Robert, and Dennis Shortelle. *From Talking Drums to the Internet: An Encyclopedia of Communications Technology.* Santa Barbara, CA: ABC-Clio, 1997.

Graham, Ian S. *Radio and Television.* Austin, TX: Raintree Steck-Vaughn, 2000.

Parker, Steve. *Lasers: Now and into the Future.* Englewood Cliffs, NJ: Silver Burdett Press, 1998.

Sachs, Jessica Snyder. *The Encyclopedia of Inventions.* New York: Franklin Watts, 2001.

Wilkinson, Philip. *Building.* New York: Dorling Kindersley, 2000.

Wilson, Anthony. *Communications: How the Future Began.* New York: Larousse Kingfisher Chambers, 1999.

Periodicals

Archaeology. Published by Archaeological Institute of America, 656 Beacon Street, 4th Floor, Boston, Massachusetts 02215. Also online at www.archaeology.org.

Astronomy. Published by Kalmbach Publishing Company, 21027 Crossroads Circle, Brookfield, WI 53186. Also online at www.astronomy.com.

Discover. Published by Walt Disney Magazine, Publishing Group, 500 S. Buena Vista, Burbank, CA 91521. Also online at www.discover.com.

National Geographic. Published by National Geographic Society, 17th & M Streets, NW, Washington, DC 20036. Also online at www.nationalgeographic.com.

New Scientist. Published by New Scientist, 151 Wardour St., London, England W1F 8WE. Also online at www.newscientist.com (includes links to more than 1,600 science sites).

Popular Science. Published by Times Mirror Magazines, Inc., 2 Park Ave., New York, NY 10024. Also online at www.popsci.com.

Science. Published by American Association for the Advancement of Science, 1333 H Street, NW, Washington, DC 20005. Also online at www.sciencemag.org.

Science News. Published by Science Service, Inc., 1719 N Street, NW, Washington, DC 20036. Also online at www.sciencenews.org.

Scientific American. Published by Scientific American, Inc., 415 Madison Ave, New York, NY 10017. Also online at www.sciam.com.

Smithsonian. Published by Smithsonian Institution, Arts & Industries Bldg., 900 Jefferson Dr., Washington, DC 20560. Also online at www.smithsonianmag.com.

Weatherwise. Published by Heldref Publications, 1319 Eighteenth St., NW, Washington, DC 20036. Also online at www.weatherwise.org.

Web Sites

Cyber Anatomy (provides detailed information on eleven body systems and the special senses) *http://library.thinkquest.org/11965/*

The DNA Learning Center (provides in-depth information about genes for students and educators) *http://vector.cshl.org/*

Educational Hotlists at the Franklin Institute (provides extensive links and other resources on science subjects ranging from animals to wind energy) *http://sln.fi.edu/tfi/hotlists/hotlists.html*

ENC Web Links: Science (provides an extensive list of links to sites covering subject areas under earth and space science, physical science, life science, process skills, and the history of science) *http://www.enc.org/weblinks/science/*

ENC Web Links: Math topics (provides an extensive list of links to sites covering subject areas under topics such as advanced mathematics, algebra, geometry, data analysis and probability, applied mathematics, numbers and operations, measurement, and problem solving) *http://www.enc.org/weblinks/math/*

Encyclopaedia Britannica Discovering Dinosaurs Activity Guide *http://dinosaurs.eb.com/dinosaurs/study/*

The Exploratorium: The Museum of Science, Art, and Human Perception *http://www.exploratorium.edu/*

ExploreMath.com (provides highly interactive math activities for students and educators) *http://www.exploremath.com/*

ExploreScience.com (provides highly interactive science activities for students and educators) *http://www.explorescience.com/*

Imagine the Universe! (provides information about the universe for students aged 14 and up) *http://imagine.gsfc.nasa.gov/*

Mad Sci Network (highly searchable site provides extensive science information in addition to a search engine and a library to find science resources on the Internet; also allows students to submit questions to scientists) *http://www.madsci.org/*

The Math Forum (provides math-related information and resources for elementary through graduate-level students) *http://forum.swarthmore.edu/*

NASA Human Spaceflight: International Space Station (NASA homepage for the space station) *http://www.spaceflight.nasa.gov/station/*

NASA's Origins Program (provides up-to-the-minute information on the scientific quest to understand life and its place in the universe) *http://origins.jpl.nasa.gov/*

National Human Genome Research Institute (provides extensive information about the Human Genome Project) *http://www.nhgri.nih.gov:80/index.html*

New Scientist Online Magazine *http://www.newscientist.com/*

The Nine Planets (provides a multimedia tour of the history, mythology, and current scientific knowledge of each of the planets and moons in our solar system) *http://seds.lpl.arizona.edu/nineplanets/nineplanets/nineplanets.html*

The Particle Adventure (provides an interactive tour of quarks, neutrinos, antimatter, extra dimensions, dark matter, accelerators, and particle detectors) *http://particleadventure.org/*

PhysLink: Physics and astronomy online education and reference *http://physlink.com/*

Savage Earth Online (online version of the PBS series exploring earthquakes, volcanoes, tsunamis, and other seismic activity) *http://www.pbs.org/wnet/savageearth/*

Science at NASA (provides breaking information on astronomy, space science, earth science, and biological and physical sciences) *http://science.msfc.nasa.gov/*

Science Learning Network (provides Internet-guided science applications as well as many middle school science links) *http://www.sln.org/*

SciTech Daily Review (provides breaking science news and links to dozens of science and technology publications; also provides links to numerous "interesting" science sites) *http://www.scitechdaily.com/*

Space.com (space news, games, entertainment, and science fiction) *http://www.space.com/index.html*

SpaceDaily.com (provides latest news about space and space travel) *http://www.spacedaily.com/*

SpaceWeather.com (science news and information about the Sun-Earth environment) *http://www.spaceweather.com/*

The Why Files (exploration of the science behind the news; funded by the National Science Foundation) *http://whyfiles.org/*

Index

Italic type indicates volume numbers; **boldface** type indicates entries and their page numbers; (ill.) indicates illustrations.

A

M

N

O

P

S

Index